P9-DGJ-884

BALLOONS!
CANDY!
TOYS!

AND OTHER
PARABLES FOR
STORYTELLERS

by
Daryl Olszewski

Published by
Resource Publications, Inc.
160 E. Virginia St. #290
San Jose, CA 95112

Illustrations: Caroline Joyce
Editorial Design and Direction: Kenneth Guentert
Typography: William Burns
Cover: Karen Dewey

ISBN 0-89390-069-9
Library of Congress Catalog Card Number 85-60241
Printed and bound in the United States 5 4 3 2 1

Copyright © 1986 by Resource Publications, Inc., 160 E. Virginia St.
#290, San Jose, CA 95112. All stories published by Resource Publica-
tions, Inc. For reprint permission, write Reprint Department,
Resource Publications, Inc., 160 E. Virginia St. #290, San Jose, CA
95112

CONTENTS

For
Rebecca and DJ

1. THE STORY TELLER'S STORY

I know you are anxious to read the first story, but be patient for a moment. If I could actually be with you right now, or if you were participating in one of my workshops, I would ask you to complete the following exercises before you heard the story. So, please complete the following exercises. Really, they are essential to the purpose of this book. I'll explain why later.

1) Imagine that you have been given the task of telling a group of catechists or any group of parishioners what it means to, "Go, make disciples." What pictures or images does "discipleship" bring to your mind? How do you think one "makes" disciples? As you think of your answer, be aware of the full image which comes to mind — the action, color, sounds.

2) Is there any character that might creatively express your understanding of what it means to "make disciples"? (Try to avoid the obviously religious ones.) Be creative! Maybe it's the garbage man, a plumber, a nurse, a used light bulb salesperson or a _____!

Thanks. That wasn't so hard, was it? Here's what I came up with.

Balloons! Candy! Toys!

"**B** alloons! Candy! Toys!" the man called out as he pushed his brightly painted cart down the street one hot summer day. A little boy heard the man's cry and rushed outside to see what it could be.

"Balloons!" There was a cloud of big balloons gently bobbing in the breeze but tied securely to the bright cart. There were red ones, yellow ones, blue ones, and green ones bouncing gently against the bright blue sky.

"Candy!" The little boy's mouth watered as he saw the large candy sticks lined up in trays on the cart. They came in all the fruity flavors — grape, orange, lemon, lime, strawberry, and cherry. And there were even large lollipops with white sugar coated candy faces painted on them.

"Toys!" All around the cart were cute, cuddly, furry stuffed animals — bears, dogs, cats, and rabbits. It was a child's paradise on wheels!

The man pushed his cart slowly past the little boy. The boy's heart sank and his head hung low for the boy did not have any money to buy the balloons, candy, or toys.

The boy waited for the man to pass and then followed him. He stayed far behind for he did not want the man to think he was going to buy something. The boy followed and listened as the man called out, "Balloons! Candy! Toys!"

The man slowly moved through the town, street by street, stopping now and then to sell some balloons, candy, and toys. And the little boy followed at a distance.

Then the man pushed his cart into the park. There were many children there, children who would like balloons, candy, and toys. But it was getting late and the little boy knew he should go back home. So the boy did not follow the man into the park.

The next day the little boy waited to hear the man's cry. "Balloons! Candy! Toys!" This time the boy did not hesitate. He followed right behind the man with the colorful cart.

As they walked down the street the little boy held out his arms and pretended he also was pushing a cart. He even said the words slowly in his head as he heard the man call out, "Balloons! Candy! Toys!" The little boy followed the man for a long time. But again it got late, and the boy did not follow the man into the park.

Everyday that summer the little boy would follow the man. And everyday the little boy would pretend he was pushing a cart and calling out, "Balloons! Candy! Toys!"

When winter came and it turned cold the man did not push his cart up and down the streets. And so the boy stayed inside and waited for summer to return.

Once again the next summer, and for many summers after that, the little boy would spend each day following the man who pushed the colorful cart and called out, "Balloons! Candy! Toys!"

After many summers the boy had grown. He was older and bigger. And so, one day, the boy followed the man into the park.

The man sold many balloons, candy, and toys in the park. And when he saw children who were poor and didn't have the money to buy anything, the man would reach into his pocket, pull out a special piece of peppermint candy and give the candy to them. The man made all of the children happy. And the boy who followed was happy also.

One day the boy followed the man all day long. He followed the man up and down more streets.

Finally, the man stopped in front of a high, old, broken fence. The man pushed the gate open and rolled his cart into the yard. Then the man stopped and turned back. The man looked at the boy who had followed him for so many summers. "Come and see," he said to the boy.

The boy came forward slowly and passed through the gate. On the other side of the fence was a small old house. The man walked slowly up the crooked steps and across the broken porch and went inside. The boy followed.

Inside the house was something the boy had never dreamed of. For there, inside that old little house, was a room filled with balloons, thousands of them, it seemed!

Wide-eyed and in disbelief the boy walked slowly through the rest of the house. Another room was filled with neatly piled boxes of candy sticks and lollipops. And there was another room that was filled from top to bottom with cute, cuddly, furry, stuffed animals. It seemed as if all the balloons, candy, and toys in the whole wide world were locked in this one little house. The boy could hardly believe his eyes!

So now the boy knew where all the balloons, candy, and toys

came from. The boy also knew that this must be the place where the man began his trip and where he finished it each day.

The man smiled at the boy and gave him one yellow balloon, one grape candy stick, and one stuffed dog. The boy felt happier than he had ever been in his whole life. The boy left that house and returned to his own home.

One day the boy again waited to hear the man cry "Balloons! Candy! Toys!" But he did not hear it. The boy waited and waited. The man did not come down the street, and the boy wondered where he could be.

So the boy began looking for the man. He ran up and down the streets. But he could not find the man.

He ran through the park. But the man was not there.

He ran to the little old house behind the broken fence. There the boy found the cart packed with balloons, candy, and toys. But the man was not there.

The boy wanted to call out for the man but realized that, even after following the man for so many summers, he did not know the man's name. So the boy called out the only names he knew. "Balloons?" "Candy?" "Toys?" he asked. But there was no answer. The man was not there.

The boy knew that many children would be sad if the cart did not come down the street. The boy knew that many children were waiting in the park for balloons, candy, and toys. So the boy did the only thing he could do.

He pushed the cart out of the yard and slowly moved it down the streets.

And every summer day after that the boy would push the cart down the streets and into the park. Every day, from that day on, the boy would make little children happy as he would cry out, "Balloons! Candy! Toys!"

* * *

COMMENTS:

What I asked you to do before you told yourself this story was to share briefly in the process which I experienced in composing it. I will try to do that in one way or another before each of the stories. I hope that by sharing these experiences you will not only be better able to enjoy the story more but also become more aware of the creative opportunities which exist around you for composing your own stories.

After each of the stories I will share some of my experiences in using the story. I hope this sharing will help you in understanding the story and perhaps, enable you to find a use for it in your own faith situation.

I originally told this story to a group of catechists who were about to begin teaching in a summer religious education program. I wanted to tell them about the importance of their role in making disciples, and I used Matthew 28: 16-20 as the basis for the reflection. But in talking to the catechists I wanted to avoid using the standard terminology by which we have come to speak about discipleship. So I used the story as a basis for our reflection. I conducted the reflection about a week before the summer program began.

Before the first day of class I continued to reinforce the image of balloons, candy, and toys by placing a balloon, a piece of candy, and a note which said, "Go, make disciples" on each catechist's desk. (I didn't have enough money to buy each one a stuffed animal, but I hoped this would be enough to get the point across.) As the catechists came to their classrooms on that first day they were visually reminded of the story and of one important aspect of their catechetical role, that of making disciples.

The catechists kept the image of the story in mind. Midway through the summer program we began planning our concluding Liturgy. The catechists suggested we use the story with the children at this Liturgy. And so we did.

In preparing for the Liturgy each class was told the story along with the Gospel upon which it was based. Each class became involved in its own preparation for the celebration. The first graders decorated a kitchen cart with helium filled balloons, candy, and crepe paper. The finishing touches were their own lovable, cuddly, animals.

The sixth graders narrated and acted out the story during the Liturgy. At the end of the Liturgy, everyone followed the cart as it was pushed across the playground to the gym where there was a concluding social.

Perhaps you can return now or sometime later to your original images of discipleship. Maybe those images could come together and be put forth in a story which you could share with others. I hope they can, for an important part of this book is not only sharing the stories but sharing the experience of each story so you might be moved to create and tell your own. Even if you never have the formal opportunity to tell those stories to anyone other than yourself, I think they will be an important part of your faith development and spiritual life.

As we journey up and down the pages of this book, I would invite you to walk behind the cart so someday you might be able to push the cart yourself and call out, "Balloons! Candy! Toys!"

Before we continue our journey I would like to point out a few things about this story which might be helpful to you in preparing your own stories. Note that this story was simple enough to be used with adults and children. Keep in mind that stories need not be complicated. Nor must one refer to a thesaurus in order to find big words to use in a story. Keep it simple, and people of all ages will be able to enjoy it.

The stories in this book use a variety of forms. This story relied primarily upon the narrative, with only the haunting refrain of "Balloons! Candy! Toys!" for drawing attention to the visual image which eventually came alive in the concluding Liturgy. Focus on a single image. The image can help others to remember the story long after it has been told. Whenever I watch a parade and a vendor comes by with balloons, candy, and toys, I am reminded of one of the meanings of discipleship and I am tempted to get up and follow along behind.

"Come and see."

2. BLIZZARD BAPTISM

I was sitting at my desk preparing a prayer reflection for a group of teachers on the readings for the Sunday of the Baptism of Jesus when I looked out my window and noticed it was snowing. It was not a gentle snow like one might imagine on a peaceful and quiet Christmas eve. No, this was the start of a full blown Wisconsin blizzard!

My eyes went back to the Gospel. How could I lead these teachers to reflect on the scene of a warm, Jordan River baptism in the middle of a cold winter?

I glanced outside. What did this snow storm have to say about baptism? How could one be baptized with frozen crystals of water which would drift three feet high and take months of Spring weather to melt?

As I continued to watch the snowflakes blow and drift against my house, I then realized they had a message about the meaning of baptism.

Snowflake

T he snowflake came down from the heavens in a winter storm along with millions upon millions of other flakes. Hurled through the sky and blown by strong winds, it gently and silently banged and bumped its way into the world.

Faster and faster the snowflake fell, not knowing where it was going, wondering where it would land, unable to change its fate. Then, with a little jerk the snowflake made a soft splash into a deep bed of other flakes. Immediately, it was bumped from behind by still more snowflakes who continued to fall helplessly on top of it.

After a long, dark, silent night the snowflakes came alive and sparkled like diamonds in the sunlight of a new day. "Where are we?" "Where are we?" The curious snowflakes asked each other the same question as they awoke.

"Mount Hermon, Mount Hermon," was the reply that echoed throughout the blown mounds of snow.

"Mount Hermon?" The snowflake wondered where *that* was. The snowflake had been to many places over many years — the Indian Ocean, Sea of Japan, the Alps. It had even been part of a typhoon which stormed Pacific islands. But it had never been to Mount Hermon.

On most days the sun would shine brightly on the mountain and melt some of the snowflakes, causing them to turn into little drops of water. The melting would make room for the other flakes and allow them to spread on down the mountain.

The snowflake waited and waited, hoping for its chance to be melted by the sun. More than anything else it wanted to escape the frozen mountain and run free as a drop of water.

As the snowflake inched its way down the icy slope it could see a little town near the bottom of the mountain. Perhaps the snowflake would be swept down into a well for drinking or into a pool for bathing. But whatever happened could only happen *if* the snowflake was melted.

That winter on the mountain seemed like one of the longest winters the snowflake could remember. The flake became impatient. It wanted to be free. It would roll and push, trying to catch a ray of sunlight that would change it from its frozen state and allow it to run down the mountainside.

One sunny day the snowflake felt warm, warmer than it had

felt in long time. It could almost feel itself glowing as it sparkled in the sunlight. The snowflake was excited. Maybe this was the day it would be freed! Then, almost like magic and in the blinking of an eye, the snowflake disappeared.

No longer a snowflake, it was now a fresh, clear drop of water.

Without wasting a minute the new water drop splashed down the mountain side and became one with other drops who had also been freed. Down and down it raced, not looking back, not wanting to be a snowflake again.

There was excitement in the flowing stream as the drop spilled over a rock and went splashing into a gurgling pool. If one could hear water drops one would have heard laughter and joy.

On and on the drop flowed. It even made it safely past the little town without being caught in a well for drinking or in a pool for bathing. It was free!

A multitude of other drops filled the stream and the stream became larger and deeper. The water drop raced with the others at feverish pace, always in a hurry, but not knowing where it was going.

One day the rushing waters of the stream slowed. The water drop gently sailed into a large body of water and became one with the bobbing waves of a sea. It felt good for the drop to relax after the long, fast paced journey down the streams.

But the sea was not always gentle. Storms would rise quickly and strong winds would blow. The water drop was bounced harshly in the churning waters of the raging sea.

The water drop learned from the older drops who had been in the sea for a long time that there was one escape from the angry sea. There was one place where the sea let out some of its water into a peaceful, lazy river. But that one place was hard to find.

The water drop, who had once escaped from the snowflake covered mountain, was determined to escape from this sea. It wiggled and splashed against the jagged shore in search of the river. Battered and bruised, it finally escaped into the river.

The river was called the Jordan. It was peaceful but unscenic. Day after day the water drop would move steadily in one direction with all other drops who made up the river. It would see only sunlight by day and stars by night.

"Where are we going?" the water drop asked a friendly wave

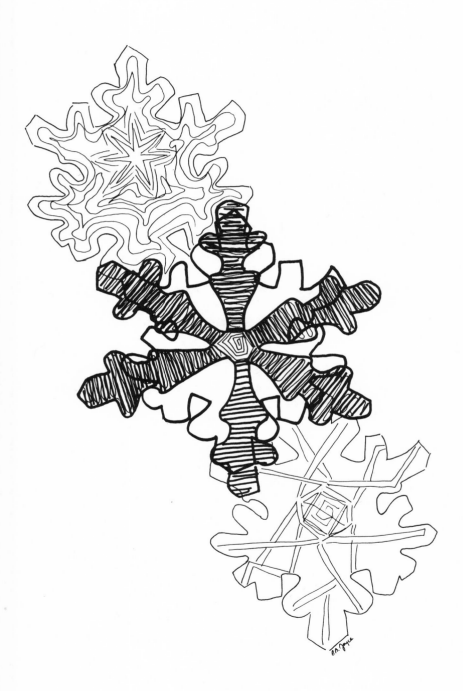

one day. "Dead Sea," the little wave answered. "Dead." "Sea." The answer came slowly, separated by the rising and falling of the gentle wave. "Dead Sea," that sounded like a terrible place to the water drop.

But the water drop was tired of running away. It was tired of escaping. So the water drop decided to simply allow the currents to carry it, along with many others, to the place called the Dead Sea.

One day, there was a disturbance in the river. The waters were spinning around obstacles in the river. The water drop, who had once fallen from the sky as a snowflake on a mountain, got caught in a swirl of water. Around and around, down and down it went.

Suddenly, the water drop was blinded by the brilliant light of the sun. It could feel something under it, lifting it out of the waters of the river towards the bright blue sky. Then it stopped.

The water drop looked down and saw that it was caught, stuck in a web of long strands of hair! And the hair was on the top of a head of a person! The drop tried to wiggle free. It wanted to escape and rejoin its friends in the river as they headed for the Dead Sea.

"Let me down! Shake your head! Do *something!*" The water drop shouted frantically in its droplet voice. But there wasn't any movement. It was only getting hotter on the head and the water drop felt a sense of hopelessness. It wished only for one quick shake that would release it and let it drop to the river below.

As the sun burned bright, the water drop became hotter and hotter. Then a cloud rolled overhead and the water drop thought it heard the cloud speak.

It was getting difficult for the water drop to breathe and the voice of the cloud became fainter. The sun was too hot! There would be no escape this time for the water drop.

And so, the once blown and drifted snowflake, who had melted and become a drop of water, evaporated.

Well, not really. For the snowflake, which had fallen on a mountain and had melted into a drop of water which travelled many miles in a river towards the sea which is called Dead, was actually ...

... transformed ...

* * *

COMMENTS:

I hope that the message of the story was clear. The story was intended to be simple and to enable the listener to identify with the various stages of development and redevelopment the snowflake experienced on its journey. In using the story with various groups I have found that people generally find it easy to identify with the snowflake. They are able to say, "Hey, I'm just like that snowflake — always wanting something more, never satisfied, always struggling, finally resigning myself to my fate, and yet refusing real conversion and unity with Christ."

I have used this story not only in discussing baptism but also with widowed, separated, and divorced groups. With these hurting people the story presents a message of hope amidst the many struggles in their lives.

The snowflake did not willingly participate in the transformation of the baptism. It was a victim of circumstances. Yet, perhaps one of the messages of the story is to encourage people to be open to the transforming opportunities available in the various circumstances of life, even those circumstances which seem to lead us to a sea which is called "Dead."

One of the characteristics of this story which allows different groups of people to enter into it is the journey motif. Almost any listener will be able to identify with the snowflake at some point in its journey. This ability to identify with the animated snowflake allows for a reflection on one's own life in a non-threatening way.

Another important aspect of the snowflake story is the image of the simple snowflake. No two snowflakes are alike, and no two people will have the same image of a snowflake. Yet, in order to see the transformation of the snowflake, one must have the simple image in mind. When I tell this story I use four large posters. One poster has the simple image of the snowflake. The second poster has a large drop of water on it. The third is blank, to show the evaporation. And the fourth has the transformed snowflake.

The technique of using the posters has a number of values. First, it helps people to visualize what you are telling them. It helps the audience to focus attention on the story and not to become distracted. Secondly, for a nervous storyteller posters provide something to literally hang on to, but not hide behind, while telling the story. Some people are very nervous when facing an audience empty handed. Thirdly, if you are nervous and afraid that you won't remember the story, you can write the story on the back of the posters and your audience will never be any the smarter!

By the way, stories are intended to be *told,* even if they are read. There is an important distinction between just reading aloud and actually telling a story. When a story is told it comes from the heart, from within the teller. Don't be afraid of missing a word or changing a part. Tell the story the way you would like to tell it. Share it in such a way that you are presenting a good friend to the audience.

This story is simple but not simple enough necessarily to be used in its entirety with children. Only children who understand the meaning of the Chi Rho and who are familiar with the Gospel passage about the baptism of Jesus will really understand the symbolic transformation of the snowflake. I have used this story with preschoolers, but I stopped at the point of the evaporation of the snowflake. I explained the Gospel passage about Jesus being baptized, and then I reassured the children that the drop of water became part of the air and would eventually return, as either another snowflake or a drop of water.

The baptism theme could then focus on changes in our lives and how we change because we have been baptized. One must be careful in using stories with children because their interpretations and understandings may not always be what ours are. While we might be reflecting on the transformational aspects of baptism, children might be frightened out of their minds about baptism causing them to disappear off the face of the earth. One must be careful to avoid the tremendous harm which could be caused by using any seemingly innocent story with young children. Always allow them the opportunity to express their feelings about the story so that if there are any fears they can be dealt with right away.

3. HEART OF STONE

I have always been intrigued by the Scripture image of a heart of stone. What does it mean to have a heart which is made of stone? How would one live with a heart of stone? What would be different about such a person's life?

What is the purpose of the heart? Medically we have come to understand the heart as the vital organ which pumps the blood to sustain our lives. Perhaps more than any other organ, the heart throughout history has been equated with life.

The heart has meant many things. We love with the heart. Our hearts can be broken when love fails, and people have died from broken hearts. The heart is the soul. We can think and understand with the heart. Perhaps, for the storyteller, it is important to *see* with the heart.

Imagine a stone that was alive, but not fully alive. Imagine a stone that was hard, round, and smooth. Imagine a stone which could speak and hear, but could not see. Imagine a stone that wanted to SEE and share in that journey ...

The Stone That Wanted to See!

O nce there was a stone which wanted to do something which no stone had ever done. More than anything else in the world, this stone wanted to see.

As most people know, stones do not have eyes. They are just hard and sit on hills or in fields or on beaches waiting to be collected, thrown, skipped, or used in building. Some stones are rough and others are smooth. Some are pretty and others are dull. But stones don't know what they look like, for they cannot see.

So one day this stone began its quest for sight by rolling down a grassy hill. It raced down the hill excitedly, bumping and banging its way merrily through the grass.

Because the stone could not see where it was going it could not avoid the rut that was in the ground. With a sudden jerking thump, it stopped. It was stuck, caught in a rut.

Before too long the stone heard a noise. "Chomp-munch. Chomp-munch." The sound was slowly moving closer to the stone. The stone recognized the sound. It was a goat eating grass on the hillside.

"Can you help me?" the stone asked the goat.

"What do you want, stone?" the goat asked as it stopped chomping at the grass.

"I want to see and I'm stuck."

"I can move you, stone, but I can't give you eyes," said the goat.

"You have eyes, goat. Tell me what you see."

The goat thought for a moment. "I see grass, twigs, and ground. Sometimes I look for water. Every day it's the same. Grass, twigs, ground. Green, brown, and more brown. It's all very boring."

Boring! The stone did not understand how seeing could be boring. The stone knew there were twigs, grass, and ground because it could feel them as it rolled. But the stone could not imagine what green and brown looked like.

The stone felt sad for the goat for thinking that seeing was boring. "Please move me," the stone asked the goat. So the goat bent down and nudged the stone out of the rut and sent it rolling on further down the hill.

The stone rolled down the hill for a long time. It rolled

through the grass, over twigs, and across the hard ground. Then it bumped into something, rolled backwards, and stopped.

The stone felt cool and knew that it must have landed in the shade. The stone sat quietly in the grass. Then it heard a familiar sound. "Chirp, chirp. Chirp, chirp." It was the sound of a bird, and the stone knew it must have landed in the shade of a tree.

"Can you help me, bird?" the stone called out.

The bird flew down from the tree. "What do you want, stone?"

"I want to see and I'm stuck in the grass."

"I can pick you up and carry you to another place, stone, but I can't give you eyes," said the bird.

"You have eyes, bird. Tell me what you see."

The bird sighed. "Everyday I see the blue sky and the tops of green trees. I look down on the leaves for bugs to eat or in the green grass for a worm. It's all blue and green, blue and green. The same thing every day. It's all very boring."

The stone wondered how seeing the sky, trees, leaves, and grass could be boring. It tried to imagine what they might look like. It tried to picture blue and green, but it couldn't because it could not see.

The stone felt sorry for the bird because the bird thought seeing was boring. "Please carry me away, bird," the stone asked. The bird picked up the stone in its beak and soared high above the trees, into the blue sky.

But the bird was not used to carrying stones and the stone was heavy. The stone slipped from the bird's beak and fell through the air. It landed with a horrible thump on the hard ground. But the stone wasn't hurt, for stones are hard.

So the stone waited and waited through the hot day and cold night, wondering where it had landed.

The next day the stone heard a sound approaching. "Clomp-clomp. Clomp-clomp." It was a burro coming down the road.

When the "clomp-clomp" was very close the stone called out, "Can you help me, burro?"

The burro stopped. "What do you want, stone?"

"I want to see and I'm stuck here on the road."
I can kick you, stone, but I can't give you eyes."
"You have eyes, burro. Tell me what you see."
The burro sighed a heavy sigh. "Everyday my back is packed with a heavy load and my head hangs low. I move slowly down the road and I see brown sand and baked clay. Sometimes the wind blows the dust into my eyes and I can't see at all. It is all very boring," the burro said with great sadness.

The stone had often felt the dust blow around it but it never knew that it was brown. It tried to imagine what dust blowing in one's eyes was like. But, of course, it couldn't, for it did not have eyes.

The stone felt sorry for the burro just as it had for the goat and the bird. They all had eyes but they did not seem to see much. The stone knew it would be different. It would see everything! And it wished it could see, just once!

"Please move me, burro," the stone asked. There was a short "clomp-clomp" and then the stone felt a sudden hit as the burro kicked the stone and sent it flying. But the stone wasn't hurt because stones are hard.

The stone bounced and bounced on the hard ground until it came to rest in a soft cushion of sand, which the stone knew was brown, whatever brown was.

One day, as the stone rested in the warm brown sand, it heard noises. These were not the noises of a goat, nor of a bird, nor of a burro. They were the sounds of people, and the people did not sound happy. The people seemed to be gathering around the stone and all of them were talking so excitedly at once that the stone could not tell what they were saying.

Amidst all the confusing noise the stone suddenly felt itself being clutched and squeezed in a large, perspiring hand. The moist fingers gripped the stone tightly but they did not hurt the stone, for stones are very hard.

The stone was full of questions. What was going on? Why had it been picked up? Why was it being squeezed so tightly? Then the stone thought it heard its name called. A loud voice seemed to shout out among all the other voices and the stone only heard part of what the voice said, "... cast the first stone!"

The stone was fearful. Were there other stones here? Why would anyone want to throw the stones? Where did they want to throw them? Oh, how the stone wished it could see!

The stone listened but heard nothing. No one was speaking. The stone felt itself being clutched even tighter by the wet hand.

But, after one last squeeze, the hand released its grip and dropped the stone into the soft bed of sand. The stone heard the people move away as they shuffled their feet through the sand.

Then the stone felt itself being pushed slowly through the sand in little circles. The pushing would stop and then start again. Something was moving the stone gently in little furrows through the sand and the stone wondered what it could be.

The movement in the sand stopped and the stone heard the voice which had spoken before ask, "Where are they? Has no one condemned you?"

Another voice was sobbing and answered weakly, "No one, sir."

The stone wished with all its might that it could see. Then it heard the first voice speak, "Neither do I condemn you. But from now on avoid this sin."

The stone thought and wondered what a sin was. It wondered if a sin was blue like the sky, or green like the grass, or brown like the sand. If only the stone had eyes, it knew it would see so as to avoid the ruts in the ground and the trees that grew near the bottom of the hill. If it only had eyes, it could even avoid sin, whatever sin was.

The wind blew the brown sand against the smooth grey stone. But it did not hurt the stone, for the stone was hard and it never saw.

* * *

COMMENTS:

The story of the stone is a sad story for the stone never sees. It is a sad story because others, who have eyes, never really see beyond the affairs of their daily existence. They never really see with the heart, and, in a sense, they all have hearts of stone.

I have used this story in Penance services. I often give everyone a stone to hold or clutch. They become one with their stones during the narration of the story. Again, I think the focus on the image is important as it helps to bring the story alive for people and helps them to identify with the stone of their own hearts.

The dialogue in the story has been carefully constructed. There is the constant imploring of the stone, "I want to see, I want to see." This has been put into the story so the listeners will also pick up the chant and say, "I want to see!" This mental refrain, it is hoped, will lead people to examine their lives, experience conversion, and seek reconciliation.

Another aspect of the story is that the goat, the bird, and the burro all express seeing as being boring. Perhaps human beings who listen to these characters might be able to say to themselves, "How silly. Seeing is exciting! Look at how much there is too see!" But do we really see everything?

It is also hoped that at the end of the story the listener will attempt mentally to define or describe what sin is for the poor stone. The listener should be able to say, "Poor stone. Stupid stone. Stupid me. I know what sin is. I have seen it. It's in my life."

Heart of Stone is a simple story, almost a children's story, but a child would have difficulty understanding the ending. However, I have used the story with children as an introduction to understanding sin. The immediate question which is raised is, "What color is sin?" Children can begin to verbalize and define their understanding of sin. If nothing else, children enjoy sharing in the journey of the stone as it bumps and bangs its way through the various experiences.

Children also enjoy the story because of the talking

animals. Even a talking stone is no problem for a child. A child's mind is filled with fantasy, a world in which the seemingly unreal becomes real. Perhaps children have an easier time seeing with the heart than sophisticated adults who have hearts of stone.

4. FOR PARENTS

I owe the idea for the following story in part to a reference made by Christiane Brusselmans in one of her presentations. Christiane was talking about the role of parents in religious education and she made reference to the Zaccheus story. She pointed out that an important element of that story was the tree, for without the tree Zaccheus would never have been able to see the Lord.

It was many years after that I had to prepare a presentation for parents about their role as the primary religious educators when I thought about Zaccheus and the tree again. That poor tree. It probably didn't want to be there in the first place, but it really didn't have any choice in the matter. That poor tree, what was its purpose in life? Did it like being climbed upon? That poor tree, it probably had no idea what was happening; it had no idea of the importance it was going to play in one man's life. Yet, there it was.

In the Zaccheus story our attention is usually drawn to the little tax collector and his conversion experience. We have heard the story so many times that we have almost lost the impact of the meaning of the story. But perhaps there is another message in the story, the message of the tree. What if the Zaccheus story could be told from the perspective of the tree?

Imagine you are a seed which is destined to become a tree. What kind of tree would you want to become? Where would you want to grow?

The Tree Near the Road

I t was in the fall of the year when the sycamore's branches were bent low by strong north winds that one seed blew off the trees with thousands of other tiny sycamore seeds in search of a new life.

The one tiny sycamore seed was blown and tossed across the harvested plains, through dried up culverts and over grassy hills in search of a place to grow.

One day the winds changed direction and the tiny seed was blown into a town. It was tossed against buildings, up over the roof tops, and down around the people on the busy road below.

Sheltered by the town, the tiny seed finally came to rest on the ground near the busy road. But it was difficult to rest for the people stepped on the tiny seed and carts rolled over it.

That night it rained and the tiny seed was soaked into the muddy earth near the busy road. There it stayed for the winter.

When springtime came the seed could feel itself gradually becoming warmer with each new day. It was warmed by the sun during the day and refreshed with rains during the night. And the seed began to grow.

The seed sprouted, popping its one single leaf through the soft, moist ground above and sending its fragile roots down deep into the earth below. No longer was it just a seed. Now it was a seedling on its way to becoming a tree.

The seedling grew quickly that summer but it had to struggle as the people continued to trample over it and carts rolled over it. But the seedling survived.

The summer turned to fall, and fall to winter, and winter to spring. The seedling sprouted some more. By the next summer it could stand firm and now was called a tree.

With roots firmly planted and branches spreading, the tree could watch the people of the busy town pass *beside* it.

As the years passed the once tiny seed, which had landed near a busy road in the town, grew and watched the people move *beneath* it.

And, as trees sometimes do, this tree wondered why it had grown near the busy road. Why hadn't it been allowed to grow in a forest or as a single tree on a sunny hillside? Why did it land here next to this busy road?

But as the young children of the town climbed upon the ever

strengthening branches of the tree to play their children's games, and as the old people of the town stopped beneath its deep cluster of leaves to escape the burning sun, the tree learned that perhaps it had grown near the busy town in order to give young children joy and old people shade.

Many more summers and winters passed. The tree grew as big as it ever would, spreading its branches further across the busy town road. The tree watched as the little children who once climbed the branches grew and became old people who now pushed their carts and stopped under the tree for the cool, refreshing shade.

And the tree was happy that it had grown near the busy road in the town.

One summer day the tree looked down and saw the people doing something unusual. They were moving to the side of the street, making a narrow path down the center of the road. The tree wondered what could be happening.

Because the tree was very tall, taller than any person in the town, it could look down the road across the town. It saw what others could rarely see. This time it saw a group of people walking, coming into town. The tree did not know much about the business of the people and it could not imagine why the road was being cleared for this group. But then, the tree really did not care.

But something caught the tree's attention. The tree noticed a little man who was trying to push his way through the crowd in order to get to the front of the line. But the people pushed and shoved the little man back and would not let him through.

The tree looked down and the tree remembered the little man. The tree remembered that as a boy the little man had climbed upon the tree's limbs, just as other boys had done. But as the other boys in the town grew taller and became men, this boy seemed to stop growing and only became a fat little man.

The tree felt sorry for the little man. No one seemed to like him in the busy town. While others talked, he was ignored. While others worked, he was avoided.

Then the tree felt something. It was a scratching and a clawing at its trunk. The tree looked down, wondering what could be going on. There it saw the fat little man trying desperately to climb the tree just as he had in his youth.

But now the man was older and heavier. He had great dif-

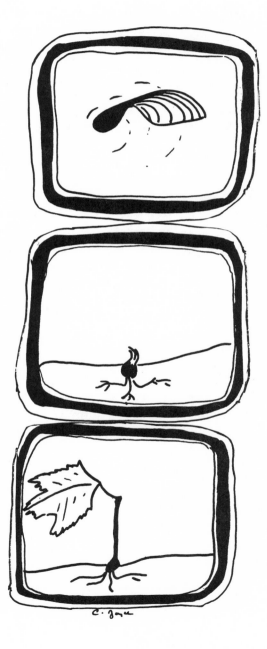

ficulty climbing the tree. Just when it seemed as if he would make it up to the bottom most branch, he would slip and fall back.

None of the people along the side of the road would help the little man. In fact, they only snickered and laughed at him when he fell down. The tree wished that it could help the little man but its branches were old and stiff and the tree could not bend even one small limb to help the little man up.

Finally, in one last desperate pull, the little man pulled himself up on the branch of the tree. The tree could feel the little man's warm breath as he huffed and puffed on the leaves. The people on the sides of the road only continued to laugh at the little man but the tree was happy that the man had made the climb.

The little man caught his breath and clung tightly to the branch as he cautiously crawled out further to get a better view of the street below.

The tree looked down and saw that the small group of people who had been walking down the road were now standing right beneath the tree. The tree had never seen these people in the busy town before and the tree had seen everyone who came and went in the town. The tree wondered who these people might be.

Then one of the men in the group looked up at the tree and called the old, fat, little man down. The little man slid backwards on the branch and then scurried down the tree just as fast as he had when he had been a boy.

The people on the sides of the busy road just shook their heads in disbelief and began to walk away. The tree did not understand. But then again, trees are not supposed to understand. They are just seeds, blown by the wind and watered by the rain, which grow to give joy to little children, shade to old people, and a place to see for those willing to make the climb.

* * *

COMMENTS:

Retelling this story here reminds me of the first time I told it. I made a crucial mistake in telling the story to that first group of parents, and I share the experience with you in the hope that you will never make the same mistake. The story was used with a group of parents whose children were preparing for first Penance. My experience with parents who are required to attend sessions in preparation for their child's reception of the sacraments has been generally that parents are, to say the least, unreceptive and hostile.

The group of parents I approached seemed to be no different. They came into the school hall barely saying a word. Few, if any of them, even smiled. They sat down, folded their arms, and gave me a look which said, "I don't want to be here. You forced me to come. Let's get this over with." I had anticipated such an audience, so I thought beginning with a story might be a good ice-breaker. Wrong!

Throughout the story the stony faces remained stony. It was as if I were standing at the bottom of the Black Hills delivering the story to Mount Rushmore. Arms remained folded. There was barely a move except for an occasional shift of the eyes which said something like, "Aw, come on!"

An unresponsive audience makes story telling a real challenge. When I am faced with such an audience I try to pull out all the stops. I try to get really excited and I attempt to become very dramatic. I try to get excited because I want the audience to get excited. Sometimes it works. But nothing seemed to work with this group, and I was devastated. I'm sure I promised myself at that time I would never tell another story. The image of giving pearls to swine came vividly to mind as I stood before this group.

I found out later from some parents who were kind enough to be honest with me that when I began the story the parents sensed I was talking down to them, so they immediately tuned out the story. What I had failed to do was to prepare the audience properly for the experience of sharing in a story.

The parents had come to the program expecting the routine dump of theology about the sacrament of Penance. They expected to hear the regular party line presented in a boring and unexciting manner. When I began with the story the parents assumed I thought they didn't have any brains at all, that I thought they weren't intelligent enough to understand a word of theology, so they felt I was treating them like children and I was talking down to them. Naturally, they resented that kind of treatment and tuned me out.

The whole misunderstanding could have been avoided if I had only taken a few moments to prepare the audience for hearing the story. In some way I should have reassured the audience that I knew they were intelligent. I should have told them I knew they had probably already heard a lot about the sacrament of Penance and I simply wanted to give them another approach to understanding their roles as parents in preparing their children for the sacrament of Penance. In whatever way I chose to say it, I should have prepared them to hear the story.

I mention this experience here because I want to caution you about telling stories. Whenever one tells a story one must be sensitive to the audience. A storyteller has to have some understanding of the audience, and must be open so the audience knows something about him or her. A few moments of warming up the audience can go a long way. Telling a story to an unreceptive audience can cause greater harm than not telling the story at all.

Even with as dismal a reception as I got with this story I had to continue with the rest of the session, for the rest of the session was built upon this story. While parents were in their session the children preparing for first Penance were in classrooms with their teachers. The children were reflecting on the Zaccheus story, but the emphasis was on the character of Zaccheus — his shortness, his rejection by the people, his desire to see Jesus, and the help he was going to need in his climb up the tree. During their session the children made little cut out figures of Zaccheus representing themselves. These were to be used later in the session.

The parents, meanwhile, after reflecting on their role as the tree, were directed to cut out trees from construction paper. On the trees the parents wrote short notes expressing how they were going to help their children to see Jesus in the sacrament of Penance. They made some pledges about specific things they would do to help their children prepare for this sacrament.

During the second hour of the program the children and parents were reunited in the school hall. There they viewed a demonstration of the rite of individual reconciliation and in the concluding prayer service the children placed the cut out Zaccheus in the paper construction tree as parents hugged their children, symbolizing their lifting them up to see Jesus.

But the use of the image of the tree did not stop there. The tree image and the Zaccheus story were used a few weeks later for the communal celebration of first Penance. A large cardboard tree was constructed and placed in the sanctuary. It was decorated with leaves made from green felt. On the leaves was written, "I have seen Jesus," along with the date of the first Penance celebration. After each child celebrated individual reconciliation for the first time, the child came forward and received a leaf from the tree as a remembrance of the event.

The use of this story became elongated. It had been used as much more than just a story. It became the focal point for understanding and celebrating Penance, and it provided a visual reminder, through the construction paper tree and felt leaves, which served to bring people back into the message of the story over and over again.

I believe stories can be more than entertaining. At their best they should serve to heighten people's ordinary experiences and draw them into a reflection on the meaning of those experiences. In using the image of the tree I hoped to project some of the questions parents often seem to have about their own roles as parents, especially in their roles as religious educators. I hope every time parents see a tree, any tree, they will be reminded in some way that they provide places to see for those who are willing to make the climb.

Perhaps it is a message which can be applied not only to parents, but to people in any state in life.

5. AN EVENING WITH JESUS

I have used the following story in more workshops and prayer services than all of my other stories combined. Part of the reason for the high mileage on this story may have to do with the way it was composed. So I think it is important that I share that experience with you now before you hear the story.

The story came about one night the day before I had to deliver a presentation to a parish adult Bible study group on the Kingdom themes in Matthew's Gospel. I was in a panic. Nothing exciting was really coming to mind. Oh, sure, I had a stock lecture prepared, but it seemed dry and boring, even to me. I knew I could probably get away using the lecture notes, but I knew I wouldn't be happy with the presentation and I suspected the audience would be politely attentive at best.

I came home from the office and I got a cold Coke from the refrigerator. I went into the living room where I sat down in my favorite easy chair. It was late at night and I was exhausted and mentally drained. I have learned that there is little work that can be accomplished in such a situation, so I resigned myself to the fact I could no longer do productive work on the kingdom themes. In the peace and quiet of that night I opened my Bible to John 3, the Nicodemus story, and I relaxed in prayer as I read: "A certain Pharisee named Nicodemus, a member of the Jewish Sanhedrin, came to him at night." (John 3, 1-2)

I immersed myself into the Gospel story. I took the part of Nicodemus and I let Jesus come to me that night in the privacy of my own living room. There I was, Nicodemus, alone at night with Jesus! He sat there on the couch, right across from me. He looked different than I had been taught to picture him. He was shorter than I had expected, and his skin was darker than I had imagined.

But there HE was, a once in a lifetime opportunity. What does one do when such a distinguished visitor really comes into one's life so unexpectedly? Stutter, stutter. "Ah. Ummm." Oh, what could one possibly say? "How about a drink?" For I knew I was going to need one! But what? Beer seemed too common. Liquor was probably forbidden. Wine? All out. I know. How about a Coke? Ya, that was it. An ice cold bottle of Coke, straight up, no ice, the all American drink. Sure. I bet he never had one before.

I ran to the refrigerator and came back in a flash. I didn't really expect it, but he was still there.

I offered and he accepted. He took a sip and smiled. So far, so good.

Okay, back to Nicodemus.

"Rabbi," I said, "we know you are a teacher come from God, for no man can perform signs and wonders such as you perform unless God is with him." Jesus gave me this answer:

"I solemnly assure you. No one can see the kingdom of God ... " (John 3, 2-3)

Wait, wait, just a minute! I've been meaning to ask you. Oh, I would like to ask you a thousand things but I got this big problem. Tomorrow I have to talk about that kingdom. What could I possibly say about the kingdom? What could I tell those fifty people about the kingdom of God that they probably hadn't heard already?

He looked at me with that type of look which makes you want to sink to the floor and quickly crawl out of a room. It was the type of look which a teacher might give you when you ask a question at the end of a class which asks exactly what the entire class has been about. It was the type of look which said, "Haven't you been listening to a thing I've said?"

Then he sighed, so I was somewhat reassured that I might get an answer, even if I hadn't been listening to whatever it was that he had been saying previously. But he looked away, off into the distance, for what seemed to be the longest amount of time I have ever known. He took a sip of the Coke and then he held the bottle, contemplating it as if seeming to wonder what in the world it was.

Then he said ...

The Kingdom of God is Like a Bottle of Coke

T ake, for example, this parable. The kingdom of God is like a bottle of Coke.

The first batch of Coca-Cola was brewed many, many years ago in a three-legged iron pot in the back yard of a pharmacy. The heavy syrup mixture was originally used as a medicine. The tonic was sold in used beer bottles, and only twenty-five gallons of the mixture were brewed in that first year.

Gradually, changes were made in the ingredients. Carbonated soda was added, and the refreshing drink was sold in more drugstores. It was a simple and humble beginning for Coca-Cola. The Kingdom of God is like that.

But word spread quickly about this popular new drink and soon, all over the country, people were asking for it by name. The Kingdom of God is like that.

From its simple beginnings Coke has now spread to the ends of the earth, today being bottled in over one hundred and forty countries. The Kingdom of God is like that.

He paused and looked at me, as if to see if I was really listening this time. My open mouth and wide eyes seemed to reassure him, and so he continued.

The Kingdom of God is like a bottle of Coke. Think of the advertising which has been used to promote it.

"THE PAUSE THAT REFRESHES."
"IT'S THE REAL THING."
"THINGS GO BETTER WITH COKE."
"HAVE A COKE AND A SMILE."
"COKE IS IT!"

The Kingdom of God is like that. The Kingdom of God is it! And more!

The exact recipe for making Coca-Cola remains a carefully guarded secret. Its mysterious ingredient, 7X, is known to only a few people, and they take extreme precautions at guarding it. The Kingdom of God is like that.

There have been many imitators but no one has been able to duplicate the taste of Coke. The Kingdom of God is like that.

He paused again and took a sip of the Coke as if to refresh himself and whet his whistle so that he would be able to continue. In fact, he even seemed to have a strange smile on his face as if surprised at himself for what he had been able to come up with.

Consider further how the Kingdom of God is like a bottle of Coke. During World War II a group of American soldiers became stranded on a Pacific island. They were thousands of miles from home, seemingly abandoned, with little hope of being found, until one day...

...a full, seven ounce bottle of Coke floated ashore!

Imagine their joy! Here at last was a sign of the homeland which they longed for. Here was a remembrance of loved ones whom they were fighting for. The Kingdom of God is like that.

The soldiers opened the bottle carefully and poured out a capfull for each of them — not even enough to wet their parched lips, but enough to fill their spirits with joy and hope! A taste of the Kingdom is like that, and more!

He was on a roll now, and there seemed to be a different presence in the room. I don't remember moving a muscle. I don't think I was even breathing as he continued.

The Kingdom of God is like a bottle of Coke. It causes people to sing — in perfect harmony!

It causes little children to share, even with Mean Joe Greene!

It gives people reason to smile!

The Kingdom of God does all that!

It is known by different names — Coke, Coca-Cola.

So is it with the Kingdom. Reign of God. Kingdom of God. Kingdom of Heaven.

One other thing about a bottle of Coke. It must be opened first before one can taste and enjoy it. The Kingdom of God is like that!

And at the bottom of the bottle is a little note: "RETURN FOR DEPOSIT."

The Kingdom of God is like that. It must be passed on and refilled so that others can also taste and see its goodness.

Seeds, yeast, treasures, pearls, feasts, a Coke ...

... the Kingdom of God is like that, and much more!

* * *

COMMENTS:

The experience of the composition of that parable is basically true, as far as I can remember it. You may choose to believe it or not. It was composed in a prayerful reflection on the eve of a presentation to a parish Bible study group which had the theme of the Kingdom of God.

The next day when I came before that class I set a full, capped, sixteen ounce bottle of Coke on a pedestal in full view of the class. As the members of the group entered the room there were a few comments and questions about the "prop" but I generally made light of them and did not immediately share the experience with them.

I delivered the stock lecture to the politely attentive group. Then, at the end of the session, I narrated the experience and the parable just as I have to you. There was a prayerful mood in that class which I have never before nor since experienced with any other group. The image of the Coke made the parables of the Kingdom come alive once again for a group which had heard them all before.

It is only fair that I share the whole experience with you in the composition of this story. I truly believe the Lord was present that night, but it was a strange set of circumstances that perhaps caused him to be there.

When I need a "mental coffee break" from my work I like to read short items, usually inconsequential, trivial, or humorous things such as those found in a book of lists or in an almanac. The history of Coca-Cola was one such article I had read in *The People's Almanac* by David Wallechinsky and Irving Wallace. I don't remember how long before the prayer experience occurred that I had read it, but it was in the memory bank of my mind.

In the prayer experience I really did turn to the third chapter of John, since that is one of my favorite Gospel passages. I like the one-on-one situation that is there, Nicodemus alone with Jesus. Some might say it was luck, others might say fate, but I must say faith caused all of the elements to come together in that experience. The reading of the almanac, the Scripture class, the theme of the Kingdom, the relaxing with a bottle of Coke, turning to the Nicodemus story — all had to be part of a power above and beyond the creative imagination of this storyteller.

An experience like that has never happened since. It may

never happen again. But I keep reading trivia, I keep teaching adult classes, I occasionally get difficult topics, I still drink Coke, and I keep on praying. Maybe, someday, a similar experience may happen.

When I use this parable in workshops or programs it often has a different beginning than the introduction I used here. I rarely share the faith experience unless it is with a group I really trust. It is not all that important to me whether people believe the experience happened. I hesitate because I do not want people's preoccupation with the introduction to interface with their listening to the parable. The parable can stand on its own as an example of a modern parable about the Kingdom.

When this parable is used in the context of a workshop on stories and storytelling I often ask participants to think of what common images Jesus might use if he were to tell the parable of the kingdom today. The most creative responses have generally come from junior high students, but so far none of them has come up with the Coke image before I tell the story.

An important element of storytelling which I see as characteristic of this story, as in previous stories, is that of a single, visual image. When I tell the story of the Coke, I pick up the bottle of Coke and hold it so people are not torn between looking at the image and listening to the story. I try to make it easy for them to do both at the same time. I do my best not to get in the way of the image. People will often forget details, they may even not remember the exact words, but people have come back to me years later and told me they still remember the image of the Coke.

Something which makes this "story" different from a traditional story is that it is not a story, as such. It does not have a plot. It has no beginning, middle, or end. Rather, the image in this parable unfolds gradually, like opening a carefully wrapped birthday gift. There is the constant reminder in the refrain that, "the Kingdom of God is like..." which is intended to evoke a "what next?" response in mind of the listener.

The climax of the story really comes after the story. In many workshops I have had a few cartons of Coke handy so that the "kingdom" can be opened and shared in a festive celebration. The audience participates in the story as they are actually able to "taste and see."

In a few instances I have had some people argue with me

about the choice of the image. They come up and tell me that
the soda pop image isn't really very good because there are a lot
of ingredients in there which are bad for our health. Somewhere
along the line they got stuck in the image and didn't allow
themselves to move beyond it. They let the image get in the way
of the message and there isn't much I can do for them.

I'm not too concerned about those criticisms because similar
criticisms could be leveled against the images Jesus used in the
Gospels. "You are the salt of the earth ... " Not exactly the best
possible image for people with high blood pressure or a heart
condition. Or, "the kingdom of God is like a merchant who
finds a pearl ... " Environmentalists could be concerned that
"kingdom seekers" will make the oyster extinct. And on and on
it could go. I present these silly examples because if you come
up with images of the kingdom and perhaps use them before an
audience, someone is bound to criticize and find fault with the
example. Don't let their criticism bother you. If the image
speaks to you, that's good enough!

Open your mind and open your eyes. Look all around you.
What images of the kingdom come to *your* mind?

6. PRIESTLY PEOPLE

Since Vatican II there has been a renewed emphasis on the priestly, prophetic, and servant-king roles which all baptized people share in union with Christ. Whenever I am asked to talk about these three dimensions I usually have great difficulty explaining adequately the priestly role, especially as it applies to the unordained. I can talk about the sacrificial aspects of priesthood and about the role of the priest as one who is set apart to lead the assembly in prayer and sacrifice, but somehow people always seem to be asking, "What does that have to do with me?" For most people it just seems to be more exciting to be a prophet or a servant-king.

One time when I was preparing a workshop on these three dimensions I specifically focused my attention on the priestly role. I was challenged by it and I wanted to make this aspect really come alive for the audience. So I reflected on some of those elements which have come to shape my own understanding of priest, beginning with Christ himself. A reflection on this role must include the basic statement which is found in the Letter to the Hebrews. But reflecting on this letter only got me further bogged down in sacrificial themes.

So I turned my attention to the last supper discourse as found in John 14, which is often labeled the "priestly prayer of Christ." The element of sacrifice is there but it also includes other dimensions of priesthood, such as prayer, discipleship, promise, hope, change, love, and friendship. With these images in mind I further reflected on what these might mean in the role of priest today. I think most people see the priestly role within the context of the ordained liturgical leader. Okay, but then what? Other questions came to mind.

Who is the priest leading?

Who are these people who gather in the assembly?

What are they like?

What's on their minds?

Why do they come?

What is the priest leading them in and for what purpose?

Where is he taking them?

How do all baptized people share in the priestly role?

One thing led to another. One image blended with another and I was able to put them all together on ... a big yellow bus! For one aspect of the priestly role is to be a ... bus driver!

The Big Yellow Bus

T he big yellow school bus was exactly on time as Mr. Elroy Johnson drove it to the corner of Beechwood and Oak at 8:15 a.m. There Mr. Elroy Johnson would pick up the last of his little riders and within exactly ten minutes the big yellow bus would conclude its appointed rounds by arriving at the front door of the Maple Grove Elementary School. At the school the bus would unload its sacred cargo of seventy-two first through sixth graders for another day of participation in what has become known as education.

"Is everybody happy?" Mr. Elroy Johnson called over the bus' speaker system as he always did when he had picked up his last passengers. It was a gloomy, grey, overcast, and cold November morning which only served to make the passengers even more depressed. So, as usual, there was a chorus of groans and moans, for these were ordinary children and none of them really liked going to school. But today was going to be different, for today those moans and groans were going to be changed into shouts of joy, cries of fear, and giggles of hope in an experience that those children would never forget.

For today, instead of turning the big yellow bus to the left to make its final run to the Maple Grove school, Mr. Elroy Johnson turned the bus to the right and drove straight out of that tiny grey town. One by one the students began to notice that they were going in a different direction. The big yellow bus passed McHenry's Hardware, Lillian's Cafe, and, finally, Hargrove's Service Station, the last building on the tiny town's limits.

The children came alive with excitement but they did not worry for they trusted Mr. Elroy Johnson as one of their best friends. As the yellow bus gently rolled down the narrow country road the children wondered where they could be going. It may have happened too quickly for anyone to really notice but as the bus rolled further and further into the countryside the grey overcast sky cleared and the sun was shining brightly like on a warm summer day. Suddenly, the brown farm fields and meadows and the barren trees were green and alive, in full bloom, like in late

August.

On and on Mr. Elroy Johnson drove that bus, up and down the narrow country roads. Then the bus came to a stop. There was a hushed silence which became interrupted by gasps of disbelief as the children peered out the windows. There, before their eyes, was one of the largest, most colorful and exciting carnivals that the children had ever seen. There was a large circus tent complete with wild animals who had been trained to do strange and wonderful tricks. There were acrobats, clowns, and jugglers. There was a large Ferris wheel, a giant merry-go-round, and games and booths to entertain any child for a childish lifetime. The children could not believe their eyes!

Mr. Elroy Johnson stood at the front of the bus and opened the door. "You may go," he said to the starry eyed children. "Everything is yours," he said with a broad smile as he waved his hands in a wide sweep of the exciting panorama. "But you must go in pairs," he cautioned, "so that no one of you gets lost."

And with that the children were off going into that child's paradise of funny clowns and circus animals. Two by two the children went throughout the fairy tale playground and they laughed and screamed with shouts of joy as they were thrilled and spilled by the dazzling spectacle of the greatest show on earth. The children forgot about school and they forgot about a depressing grey overcast November day. They only knew the now, a timeless, spaceless, cotton candy land of forever.

But even fairy tale circuses do not last forever and almost in unison, at some unknown time, and beckoned by some unheard call, the children returned to the big yellow bus. Two by two they came from the four corners of the giant playground. They returned and boarded the big yellow bus that was destined to carry them to the Maple Grove Elementary School.

As the big yellow bus prepared to leave Mr. Elroy Johnson looked back at the exhausted passengers. "Is everybody happy?" he asked. There was a loud chorus of affirmative answers as everybody was indeed happy, happier than they had been in a long, long time. And so the big yellow bus moved on further down the narrow country

road.

The bus rolled merrily on and on, up and down the country roads, around and around the winding farm meadows, further and further away from the tiny town of Maple Grove.

Suddenly, the big yellow bus slowed and turned off the narrow country lane going down one of the bumpiest, rockiest, ruts of a road in the entire county. There were gasps of fear from the little children as they recognized the road. For the road was the very one which led to the house of none other than the wicked Wanda Nargoose!

All of the children knew that the wicked Wanda Nargoose was a witch, at least that's what they had been told. They had heard that she would fly on her broom whenever the moon was full, and from the safety of their bedroom windows they would often watch for her. But, of course, none of them had really ever seen her. They had heard that she was one of the most wicked, terrible, and ugliest persons ever to have walked the face of the earth. But worst of all, they had heard that the wicked Wanda Nargoose had a large iron pot which she used to boil little children so that she could eat them for supper!

The children were jostled in their seats as the bus slowly inched its way down the bumpy, rocky road past crooked, gnarled trees which seemed to bend their long branches down hungrily at the big yellow bus. The bus slowly moved past painted red signs that warned the children to keep out and turn around before it was too late, whatever "it" was. But the bus moved on and ignored the warnings. Then the bus stopped.

Fearfully, the children slowly raised their tiny heads from behind the protection of the padded bus seats. Their eyes opened wide and their skin turned white for they expected to see a huge, vine-covered haunted house of fairy tale witches. Instead, they saw a small, dilapidated, unpainted, run-down shack of a house. The roof of the little house sagged and the front porch was broken and leaning forward, as if ready to tip over on top of them. From one half-broken railing of the old porch three big black cats raised their furry tails and glared their big yellow eyes at the strangers.

The children's widely opened eyes moved slowly across the haunting landscape. Then, a large singular gasp came from the mouths of the seventy-two children as at once they noticed a big iron pot on three legs standing to one side of the run down shack. The children quickly ducked down behind the seats again.

A voice boomed over the speakers in the bus, "Is everybody happy?" Mr. Elroy Johnson asked the question in the same tone which he always used. There was no response from the children for indeed, no one was happy. Then Mr. Elroy Johnson looked at the frightened seventy-two children and he told them, "Remember the circus!"

With those words of reassurance, which were not at all reassuring to the children, Mr. Elroy Johnson opened the door of the big yellow bus and bounded off onto the dusty yard in front of the spooky little house. Mr. Johnson seemed comfortable here and he busied himself by taking cans of paint, brushes, hammers, nails and all kinds of material needed to fix up a house from the tool compartment beneath the bus.

The children slowly and reluctantly began to file off the big yellow bus. They stopped at the door, glanced cautiously in all directions, and then ran next to Mr. Elroy Johnson. The nearest empty hand was immediately given paints and brushes. Some were given hammers and nails. Without barely a word Mr. Elroy Johnson directed the children to various places and assigned them to their tasks. Some went to the back of the shack, others went to the sides, and most attempted to stay in the safety of the front. "Remember the circus!" Mr. Elroy Johnson shouted encouragingly. There was a slow dipping and flopping of brushes as the children began to paint the little house.

The seventy-two children and Mr. Elroy Johnson worked in the eerie silence which was interrupted only by the flapping of brushes and pounding of nails. Stroke by stroke the children spread bright yellows, pinks, and blues over the little house of the wicked Wanda Nargoose.

As the bright colors became larger and larger the children began to giggle, for indeed some of them did remember the circus. The bright colors began to take the shapes of balloons, cotton candy, and large circus animals.

The children painted faster and faster as the images of the circus once again came alive through their work.

But the slightest unexpected noise would cause the children to jump in fear for any moment they expected to feel the long, sharp finger nails of the wicked Wanda Nargoose grabbing their little bodies so that she could throw them into her big boiling pot.

As the children worked they noticed smoke coming from the old chimney of the house and the children stopped to sniff. As they wrinkled their noses they could smell a pleasant aroma, not the stench which they had expected from a witch's brew. But pleasant aroma or not, the children quickened their pace, working faster and faster, for they did not want the scraggly haired, prune-faced woman in the long black dress to catch them painting her house with circus pictures.

At last the job was done and the children hurried to the front yard of the house. They huddled safely around Mr. Elroy Johnson. There they stood, admiring their completed masterpiece. There was a sense of pride in the children as they admired the brightly painted house which no longer looked haunted and no longer looked dilapidated. If one looked closely at the children, one would probably even have seen a smile on their faces for indeed, they had remembered the circus.

But then a shrill, spine tingling fear came over the seventy-two little children as the front door of the old house opened slowly. The old door creaked on its rusty hinges and the children huddled tightly against each other in great fear. What would come out of the house?

The door opened wider and a woman appeared in the doorway. Tongues got stuck in parched throats and little fingers tightly clutched the person nearest them as the children awaited the appearance of the wicked Wanda Nargoose.

From out of the shadows of the dark house the woman came out slowly onto the front porch. She was carrying a large tray. The children closed their eyes in unbelievable fright, for they were sure that there was a human head on the large tray! But the woman was carrying a large tray of freshly baked gingerbread cookies! The children stood frozen in fear as the woman came slowly down the steps of the porch towards them.

Then the children noticed something strange. As the woman stepped into the bright light, the children noticed that Wanda Nargoose did not have long scraggly black hair. They noticed, much to their surprise, that her skin was not shriveled. And they noticed that the woman did not have long sharp nails. In fact, the children did not think that the woman looked like a witch at all.

Instead, what the children did see was a woman who had blond hair, brown hair, and black hair that was neatly cut in a fashionable style. They noticed that she had blue eyes, green eyes, brown eyes, and hazel eyes. They saw that her skin was fresh, clean, and soft. And they saw that the woman wore a blue suit, a red skirt and white blouse, a pastel colored dress, and seventy other types of clothes. For the children saw not the wicked Wanda Nargoose. No, what each saw as each gazed in the eyes of the woman carrying the tray of freshly baked gingerbread cookies was the image of ... his or her own mother!

No one remembers boarding the bus and no one remembers the bus driving away from that freshly painted scene; but as the bus moved down the country road again there were cookie crumbs on the laps of the little children.

The voice of Mr. Elroy Johnson was again heard over the speakers of the big yellow bus. "Is everybody happy?" he asked as usual. There was no response, for the little children did not know if they were happy or not. To be sure, they were relieved to have somehow escaped from the place where they thought lived the wicked Wanda Nargoose.

The big yellow bus rolled on merrily, continuing its strange journey through a land of disbelief. And for a third time in its timeless journey, the bus again stopped. This time it stopped on the top of a grassy hill. The children looked out and beyond them, down at the bottom of the hill, they saw a Mark Twain swimming hole, a child's delight of cool fresh water on a hot summer day. "Remember the circus!" shouted Mr. Elroy Johnson as he opened the school bus door and ran on ahead of the children, making a large cannon ball splash as he jumped into the cool water.

There were screams and giggles of excitement as the happy children followed the bus driver down the hill and splashed their way into the refreshing waters of the pool. The waters stirred with the playful splashing and swimming of the little children.

Finally, dripping wet from head to toe, the exhausted children stretched themselves out on the grassy banks where they dried in the hot summer sun. There they ate a picnic lunch and drank ice cold lemon aide. Then they once again boarded the big yellow bus.

The bus rolled on and on across country road and it was exactly 8:25 a.m. when the big yellow bus pulled up in front of the door of the Maple Grove Elementary School on a grey, overcast, cold November morning. As the bus stopped the voice of Mr. Elroy Johnson boomed over the speakers and asked, "Is everybody happy?"

There was a long pause. Children looked at each other with the same questions on their minds but afraid to ask each other. But then, as if responding to some unseen signal, the seventy-two gave a loud, unified affirmative cheer which was shouted so loudly that the whole world knew they were indeed the happiest children who ever lived.

Mr. Elroy Johnson smiled in satisfaction. "Good!" he said. "Now make others happy!"

There was the shuffling of little feet as the children made their way to the front of the bus. As the children moved to the door they peered down at the driver's seat, the very spot where Mr. Elroy Johnson sat as he drove the big yellow bus. But Mr. Johnson was not there. Nor was he standing outside the bus. He was nowhere to be seen, ever again.

But the children remembered him. They remembered the circus. They remembered that day. And they remembered the words of Mr. Elroy Johnson and they did try to make everyone happy.

* * *

COMMENTS:

So, you are probably wondering what in the world does that story have to do with our sharing in the priestly role of Christ. I'll lead you through it and give you my explanation, but feel free to accept it or reject it. Maybe, though, it will open up some new understanding of the meaning of our priestly roles.

I see the priestly role as primarily being one which leads others in the celebration of covenant. But not only does the priest lead the celebration of covenant. More importantly, the priest helps people to experience and make covenant, the one covenant, the New Covenant. How was covenant made and celebrated in the story?

First of all, covenants are generally made with unsuspecting or unwilling participants. Noah, Abraham, and the entire group of Hebrews in Egypt either were unsuspecting of how their involvement in an experience was going to lead to covenant or were, to various degrees, unwilling to participate in it. There was no vote taken among the Hebrews in Egypt, for example, to see how many wanted to journey out into the desert. If there had been a vote, there probably would not have been a unanimous decision to go forth. God does not offer the people a choice. He does not say, "Do you want me to be your God?" Rather, he drags everyone into the event, like it or not. Jesus did not ask, "How many of you want to be saved?" Rather, he simply said, "This is it! This is the new covenant for all." Period.

Becoming involved in a covenant experience is a lot like boarding a bus for school. No one asks if you want to go to school. You are simply sent out to the corner to wait the arrival of the bus. You board the bus and it moves you to school. That's it. The seventy-two children from Maple Grove were like the Hebrews, unsuspecting of what was about to happen and perhaps even unwilling to participate. But they went along for the ride.

But being unsuspecting and unwilling does not automatically guarantee full participation in the covenant. There may have been some students on the big yellow bus who kept their eyes closed during the whole ride. There may have been some who refused to get off the bus to go to the circus, to help paint the house, or to go swimming. There may even have been those who came to the end of the ride and would say, "I didn't see anything, I didn't hear anything." For these there was no real covenant, although they had the opportunity to share in the full benefits because of the experience which had been thrust upon them.

A second characteristic of covenants is that they are salvific acts. They are experiences which lead people from a good to a better or from slavery to freedom, from death to new life, from the boredom of school to a day at the circus, from the fear of Wanda Nargoose to a new outlook on life.

Because of the salvific experience people should no longer be afraid. People know the mighty forces of evil have been overcome, and they can be overcome again. And people know this not vicariously but through a genuine, personal experience. People are not just told they can be born again, they actually live new lives. The children were not just told there was nothing to fear about Wanda Nargoose: she actually served them cookies!

The saving activity which is part of the covenant experience leads to joy, celebration, and refreshment. It leads to such celebrations as Passover, Eucharist, or a dive into a cool, refreshing swimming hole on a warm summer day.

Thirdly, within the salvific experience of the covenant, directions are given. There is some mandate from the covenant maker to carry out the experience of the salvific act of the covenant. "Gather your children and tell them..." "I am the Lord your God...you shall..." "Take and eat." Or, "Make others happy!"

And this leads to a fourth characteristic which involves the remembering, retelling, and re-experiencing of the covenant. The experience is so intense that it begs to be experienced again and again. The experience is so dramatic that others need to hear of it.

What then does all of this have to do with the baptized person's sharing in the priestly role? Well, I think each baptized person has the potential for being a bus driver, a Mr. Elroy Johnson. Perhaps some have greater potential for expressing this role than others. Maybe some are in better positions to be bus drivers as they have ready-made groups to lead, such as parents who have their children, teachers who have classes, workers who have fellow employees.

My own experience with catechists, for example, is that generally they have groups of unsuspecting and unwilling participants at their beck and call. They also usually have groups that are in need of salvation. As a priestly participant the catechist is a bus driver. One option for the catechist is to drive the bus on its appointed rounds, paging through the text book like the clock-work stopping and starting of the bus, making sure that one stays on the schedule so that, at precisely the last minute of the last day of the last class, the final word of the last chapter will have been read. Everyone will be on time but few, if any, will have experienced covenant.

Another option for the catechist who takes seriously the priestly role is the one presented in the story. Turn a different corner occasionally and take the unsuspecting and unwilling participants on a salvific experience. The students are not given a choice. Mr. Elroy Johnson did not take a vote. There is no democracy in covenant-making. It is simply this: "I will be your teacher and you will be my students and away we go!"

Please do not misunderstand. It is not my intention in using this example from the story to advocate taking students on a field trip every week. What the bus driver must do, in whatever situation one is in, is lead the unwilling and unsuspecting participants into a salvific act which can be the basis for covenant-making. Catechists need to ask, "What enslaves my students?" All baptized people who want to share in this priestly role need to ask, "What are the Wanda Nargooses of other people's lives and how can I help them to overcome these?" What experiences can help save others from their enslavements?

The priestly covenant-maker has to do more than just talk about freedom. Preaching is not enough. The priestly role involves living out the prophetic role. Mr. Elroy Johnson could have driven the big yellow bus past Wanda Nargoose's house and said, "See, boys and girls, you don't really have to be afraid. She's not so bad." But instead, he drove them straight into the fear and led them on a salvific experience which helped them to overcome those fears.

Sometimes the salvific experience can be planned in advance and controlled. Such was probably the case of Mr. Elroy Johnson, who had given some thought to what he was going to do that day. He came prepared with paints and brushes, for instance. But at other times, the experience may arise and suddenly be there. A dramatic experience, such as a death, may often reveal a group's fears about dying. The priestly role is to drive the bus straight into that situation and help save others from those fears. The bus driver who is overly concerned about schedules and promptness will probably avoid such situations in order to stay on schedule.

One has to be sensitive to the fears of others, to those things which enslave them and hold them back from loving God and loving others. One need not be a catechist or have a formal position of religious leadership in order to exercise the priestly role. There are many enslavements among family members, co-workers, fellow members of the communities in which we live, and in the world-at-large. There is a good job market for bus drivers, for covenant-makers.

The role of the bus driver is not limited merely to driving the bus. One must also be able to summarize the experience, give directions, and be able to explain the meaning of the experience so the participants can go forth to live new lives. People should be directed to "make others happy," or something similar, because of the experience.

Salvific experiences are not just fantasy. They are not just fabricated stories. Eventually the riders have to come back to the door of reality so they can celebrate the meaning of the ride and share it with others. No need to worry about schedules. The bus will probably arrive at exactly 8:25 a.m. anyway. And if it doesn't, so what?

Finally, it is important to note that covenant experiences by themselves do not necessarily build community. Rather, the potential for people to form community exists because of a covenant experience. All people are saved. All the children rode the bus. But they were just a group of children who happened to share the same ride. At the end of the ride they could choose never to see each other again. They could choose never to talk to each other about their experience. We don't know what they chose to do.

Perhaps, because of the experience on the bus, the children may have eaten lunch together at school and talked about the ride. They may even have asked each other, "Did you see what I saw?" They may have sought support from each other and affirmation of their experiences. Maybe the children would even continue to gather together to celebrate and relive the experience. Some would probably choose not to participate in the community experience, and maybe the number of those who did gather to celebrate the event would gradually diminish over the passing days, weeks, and years. But for as long as two or three of them band together to recall the experience, they will be forming and living out a community based on that experience.

One final note on this explanation of the story and its application to understanding the baptismal participation in the priesthood of Christ deals with the role of the ordained priesthood. If the priestly role is that of covenant-maker, what then is the role of the ordained priesthood? Continuing with the image presented in the story, the role of the ordained priest is to serve as a leader of the assembly of all the different bus riders, all the different covenant communities who wish to come together to celebrate the one covenant, the New Covenant. There is nothing to say that other covenant-making experiences did not happen on the other buses coming to school that day.

The liturgical role of the priest, the leader of the assembly of covenant communities, is to gather these communities together festively (take them to the circus), drive them straight into the heart of their enslavements (Wanda Nargoose), and lead them out of that enslavement so they are refreshed (swimming hole) in order to be empowered to live their lives differently (make others happy.) What the ordained priest does for the assembly of communities, every priestly person should be doing at the local level — at home, at work, and in the market place. Priestly people give others a reason for wanting to come together to celebrate all their individual covenant experiences.

Covenant-making experiences will not happen dramatically every day of one's life. In fact, there may be few such experiences in one's lifetime. Perhaps most people spend their lives being riders rather than drivers, unsuspecting and often unwilling participants but with great potential before them. Even if people spend most of their time being riders, they can still lean over in their seats and say to the person next to them, "Hey, look at that!"

A story such as this one can form the basis for understanding a difficult concept. The story provides a focal point for understanding and further discussing the concepts involved. Too often the approach in teaching-preaching is, "Today I would like to talk about, ... " followed by a statement of the topic and numeration of the points related to it. But there is no creative image to focus on. The use of a story helps to create a mental image which will probably be remembered longer than the specific points of the lecture.

This particular story about the big yellow bus has been used only with adults, but I hope it shows that a story can be used to help explain almost any difficult concept to almost any age group. If we are a priestly people, if we are bus drivers, then we might do well to follow the example of those who are really bus drivers. Some of the most enjoyable and memorable rides on buses have been those on which the bus driver was friendly and provided a commentary on life through the telling of stories, anecdotes, and parables.

One last thing I would like to share is how I have used this story. Sometimes, when this story is used in a workshop, I prepare little yellow buses cut out of construction paper. I distribute these before telling the story, and I ask participants to think of some people they know and to write down on one side of the paper bus some of the things that enslave these people, the things which hold them back from entering into loving relationships. I then ask people to write a short note on the other side of the bus expressing where they would like to drive the bus in order to help these people become free and able to overcome their enslavements. After the narration of the story and the explanation of it, participants can again look at their buses and perhaps have a sense of their potential priestly role as bus drivers. The next step is for people to go out and drive the bus.

Who are some of your bus riders?

What enslaves them?

Where would you want to drive your bus in order to free them and help them enter into a covenant relationship?

7. FROM HOSTILITY TO HOSPITALITY

What words come to mind when you see the word *hostility?*
What images or symbols come to mind in thinking about
hostility?
What are some of the most hostile acts people do to others?
What are some objects people use in being hostile?
What words come to mind when you see the word *hospitality?*
What images or symbols come to mind in thinking about
hospitality?
What are some ways which people can best express
hospitality?
What are some objects people use in being hospitable?

Hostility. Hospitality.
Is there any image or symbol which can be both a sign of
hostility and a sign of hospitality? Can an image of hospitality
be transformed into an image of hospitality? How?

The Gift Of The Doors

O nce upon a time, a long, long time ago, in the far-away land of Ephata, people lived in huts and caves. It was such a long time ago that the people did not even have any doors on their huts and caves. And because the people of Ephata had no doors, they could move freely from hut to hut and poke their head in to say a friendly, "Hello," stop to chat awhile, or even be invited in to share a meal, to tell stories, to laugh, and to love. Everyone was very friendly in the land of Ephata, the land without doors.

But, of course, there were problems in not having doors. During the summer the doorless huts would let in the rain and bugs. And the cold winds and snows would blow through the openings during the long winters.

So, one day, the wise and loving king of the land visited Ephata. The king felt sorry for the people who had to live with the bugs and rain, the cold winds and snows. So the king brought the people of Ephata a gift. He brought them the gift of a door — a bright new sturdy oak door, made from the finest wood to be found in the forest and trimmed with the shiniest brass hinges and locks.

The people of Ephata gathered around the king and there was great excitement as the kindly king showed the people how to frame a door and how to hang it properly on its hinges so that it would swing freely. The king even showed the people how they could build other doors so that everyone would have a door. The people of Ephata were happy and they danced in the streets as they celebrated the gift of the doors which the kindly king had brought them. The people rejoiced for no longer would they have to endure the pesty bugs of summer and the cold blowing snows of winter.

The citizens of Ephata immediately ran out into the woods which surrounded their town and they chopped down trees so that they could build doors to cover all of the caves and huts. They chopped down the oak trees, the maple trees, the walnut trees, the fir trees, and the hickory nut trees. Then they cut down the apple trees, the peach trees, the pear trees, and all the fruit bearing trees of the forest. They even cut down all of the vines and bushes in the forest. Day by day all of the people of Ephata labored, cutting, planing, sanding, nailing. Finally, after many days of hard work, all of the doors were in place. Every hut and every cave was enclosed with a solid door. And the people of Ephata were proud of the work they had done and they praised the king for the gift he had given to them.

As the people stood in the street admiring the row upon row of beautiful doors, their eyes suddenly looked beyond the town and the people gasped! For the first time in many days the people realized that in their enthusiasm to build the doors they had cut down ALL of the trees of the beautiful forest!

Everything was gone! No longer would the people have nuts and fruit to eat. And because the trees were gone, so were the birds and all of the animals who once lived in the beautiful forest. The people panicked for they quickly realized that all of their food was gone and they would now suffer a great famine.

The once friendly people who had been happy for the gift from the king now became angry. They cursed the king. And in rage they ran to the spot where their beautiful forest had been and they quickly picked up the nuts and fruit which had fallen to the ground.

They ran and stumbled as they raced back and forth from the forest to their homes, carrying as much of the remaining food as they could. The once friendly people pushed and shoved each other in a massive stampede as they hoarded the little food that was left.

When all of the nuts, fruit, and berries were picked cleanly off the ground the people ran quickly to their huts and caves to lock their doors, the new doors which the king had taught them to build from the wood of the forest. They bolted the doors and braced them tightly so that no one else could enter to take the food which they had salvaged.

The once friendly people locked each other out. They even slammed their doors on the king and locked him out. Through the bolted doors one could hear the people shouting in anger at the king for what he had done to the people.

No longer were the people of Ephata open and friendly to each other. No longer were their doors open to each other. The poor king who had given the people the wonderful gift of the doors would walk up and down the empty streets, knocking on the solidly built and firmly locked doors trying to get the people to open their doors. "Open up! Open up!" he would shout to the people of Ephata. But the people would not open their

doors, not even to a king. The people would only shout back, "Go away! Go away!" And they never let the king in.

The doors of Ephata were tightly closed. No longer would they open to welcome a stranger. And with tightly closed doors the once friendly people even stopped talking to their neighbors and friends. The once friendly and open town of Ephata was now sealed silent like a tomb.

Even inside the houses of Ephata the people became hostile to each other. With some of the remaining wood that the people had salvaged from the forest they built even more doors. They hung a door in every part of their house. They hung a door to separate brother from sister, wife from husband, and parent from child. Each person retreated further and further into a corner of the house behind a tightly locked door.

And with the last remaining chips of wood which the people had shaved off their doors they built little doors. They built little doors to place over their ears so that they would not have to listen to each other if they did not want to. They built little doors for their eyes so that they would not have to see each other even if they had their eyes open. And they even built little doors which they placed over their hearts so that they no longer would have to love each other.

The king was sorry for ever having given the people the gift of the doors. After many years the king stopped visiting the hostile town and instead, every year, the king would send a royal messenger to the town. The royal messenger would walk up and down the empty streets, banging on the doors, begging the people to open their doors. He would shout out, "Open up, in the name of the king!" But when the people of Ephata saw the royal messenger they would close the doors on their ears so that they would not have to listen to his message and they would close the doors on their hearts so that they would not have to welcome him. Without hearing him, the people would only shout back at the messenger, "Go away! Go away!"

It was many, many years after the gift of the doors had been given by the king to the people of Ephata that the king one day decided to send his son, the crown prince, to the tightly sealed town. The prince walked up and down the streets, banging on the doors and shouting, "Open up! Open up" just as his father had and just as the royal messenger had. But, as usual, the people would not listen and they only shouted back angrily,

"Go away! Go away!"

And so the prince went away.

But the prince returned a few days later. He said nothing and he did not even try to knock on any of the doors. Instead, the crown prince came into town carrying one of the biggest, strongest, most beautifully constructed doors that had ever been built. He walked slowly into the town with the heavy door on his strong young back. Walking right into the middle of the town the prince placed the door down on the ground in the town square. Then the prince left.

But the prince came back in a short while. This time he was rolling four large boulders down the street. With his massive young hands the prince rolled the boulders to the very spot where he had placed the huge door. Then the prince picked up the door and placed it on the four boulders so that the four boulders were directly beneath the four corners of the door. He leveled the door to make sure that it did not wobble and when he was satisfied he left the town of Ephata once again.

After a few days the prince returned to the town. This time he was pulling a large wagon, a wagon so large that it would have taken a team of oxen to pull. But the prince was young and strong and he could easily pull the wagon down the street.

Those people of Ephata who dared to open the doors of their eyes saw that the wagon was filled to overflowing with nuts, berries, and fruit. The wagon was heaped with more than enough fresh food to feed all the people in three towns the size of Ephata.

The prince pulled the wagon to the spot where he had put the large wood door on the four boulders. Slowly and carefully he began to unload the wagon, spreading the nuts, berries, and fruit on the door. But as large as the door was, it was much too small to hold all the food the prince had brought into the town.

So the prince left the town again.

The next day the prince returned. This time he was pulling another wagon. This wagon was filled with boulders and large stones. The prince pulled the heavy wagon slowly down the street and stopped. Then he took the stones out of the wagon, slowly, laboring for days in order to place all the large stones in two straight rows down the center of the main street in Ephata.

When he was finished the young prince stopped and looked at his work. He was pleased. From one end of the door which the prince had placed on the four boulders came two rows of evenly spaced stones down the center of the town road.

Now the prince was very hungry from all of the work he had been doing. So the prince sat down at the door on the four boulders and he began to eat the nuts, berries, and fruit which he had placed on it.

The people in the enclosed huts and caves who had dared to open the doors of their eyes watched in amazement at this strange activity. Their mouths watered at the sight of all the food. They wondered why the prince had made the two rows of stones but they were afraid to ask anyone for they still had the doors over their hearts closed.

However, some of the people who dared to look out of their windows realized what had happened. For when they dared to open their eyes and look beyond the tiny town of Ephata they saw that there was once again a forest surrounding the town. The forest which had once been cut down in order to make doors for all of the nuts and caves had now regrown. Once again the forest had nuts, berries, and fruit to eat. Even the birds and animals had returned.

Without saying a word to each other the people of Ephata carefully and cautiously began to take down their doors. First they took down the doors over their eyes so that they could see. Then they took down the doors over their ears so that they could hear. Then some bravely took down the doors over their hearts and then they realized that they loved the prince. They even noticed that they once again even loved their neighbors.

With a flurry of excitement the doors of the huts and caves were ripped off their hinges and taken out to the center of the street where they were placed on the two rows of stones which the prince had neatly set out in the middle of the town.

Eventually, all of the doors were taken down and set upon the stones so that from one end of the town to the other the wood panels formed one long table which became filled with nuts, berries, and fruit.

As the people gathered around the long table to celebrate a feast they began to talk to each other again. They were friendly and they even shared the food with each other. The people of the town had become so friendly that they even invited the king, the kindly king who had given them the gift of the doors, back to the town. And the king came back and sat at the head of the

table with his son, the prince. The people cheered, "Long live the king and praise to his son, the prince!"

The people of Ephata stayed around that table for a long time. Once again they ate together, talked, shared stories, hugged and kissed each other. Strangers who would come into the town were once again greeted with warmth and love and would be seated around the long table in the middle of the town so as to share in a meal.

Many, many years have since passed. No one is even alive to remember the day when the king first brought the gift of the doors to that far away place. Today the people use their doors only to keep out the summer rains and to fend off the winter winds. For the doors hang loosely so that they can be taken down to make a table to share a meal whenever family, friends, and neighbors gather together.

* * *

COMMENTS:

The image of a door was selected for this story because it was one image which surfaced when I answered the questions posed before the story. Also, it is an image which is common to all people's experiences. Everyone has a door! Doors are everywhere. And the image of a door is one which can express both hostility and hospitality. Doors can be shut (hostility) or they can be opened (hospitality).

This story was told at a parish Advent communal penance celebration and was intended to help people reflect on how they could change the hostilities of their lives into movements of hospitality, especially at the Christmas season. But I think the story has more than a penitential theme. I deliberately put a Eucharistic theme into the story as well, as shown by the doors becoming tables. The doors of hostility not only need to be opened, but they need to be taken down and set upon stones as banquet tables so that others can gather to share in the meal of friendship and love. In other words, true repentance leads to Eucharist.

When this story was used in the communal Penance services it was divided into two parts with a reading from Jeremiah and a reading from Matthew coming between the two parts. I liked the idea of dividing the story, but I'm not sure the readings from Scripture were effective. In fact, I think the Scripture readings added too much to the service. Perhaps a silent meditation, a song, recorded music, or even a simple Psalm response might have been more effectively used as an intermission.

This story is almost too long to be used in a Liturgical setting. But when I was given the assignment to compose it I was told it could be "homily length." That sure was open-ended! Also, since the story was the focal point of the service, and no other homily was to be given, I took the liberty of extending the story beyond what I consider a comfortable limit for liturgical stories.

In preparing the story I told it to my daughter, who was five years old, and she listened to it, enjoyed it, and even seemed to understand it on her own level. So I wasn't too concerned about the length, for I figured if a five-year-old could stay awake through it most adults probably would also.

I would like to interject something here about preparing and practicing the telling of stories. I generally try to make the stories as simple as possible, using single images and concise language. In fact, I try to write my stories with my own young children in mind.

I usually try to practice telling my stories by using them as bedtime stories with my children. If the child is still awake and attentive at the end of the story, I feel some assurance that the story isn't boring. If the child is sound asleep, I head back to the typewriter.

I know my children do not understand the theological messages of the stories, but I am not concerned about that. My theological messages or morals are aimed at adults who can, supposedly, better understand those thing. If my children at least remember the images of the story, then I basically consider the story to be successful.

I once had a cuddly, stuffed bear named Emil who was loaned to me by a friend. I placed Emil in a chair on the other side of my desk in my office. A couple of ideas for stories came to mind while Emil was visiting, so I tried the stories out on the bear. I figured if Emil could understand them, then anyone could.

During one recitation of the stories I got carried away. I lost eye contact with Emil and raced on and on, reading from the script. After a while I looked up and I noticed that Emil was standing on the chair, looking out the window, obviously oblivious to my creative narrative. Needless to say, that manuscript was scratched!

The adage that everyone likes a story just isn't so. Perhaps it should be restated, "Everyone likes a good story." One of the distinctions between a story and a good story is that a good story is written and rewritten, rewritten, and rewritten. An important aspect in telling a good story is practice. Don't wait to get in front of an audience before telling your story for the first time. You may find them standing on their chairs looking out the windows, just like Emil. If you don't have little children of your own to practice your stories on, rent some from a neighbor or a friend. If nothing else, go to a carnival and try your luck at winning a stuffed animal who can become your own personal critic.

One final note about this story. I have used this story as a follow-up story to the previous one, as a way of further clarifying the priestly role discussed in that story. In this story the priestly role is expressed through the prince who prepares a banquet for the people and shows them how to be released from their enslavement. The prince does more than just talk, he acts. He sets a table before them and allows them to enter into the celebration of the birth of the new forest.

8. PUT ON A HAPPY FACE!

I was struck by a line in one of the Psalms (I don't remember which one and I don't remember the whole situation) but the line spoke about people living in "houses of gloom." I was struck with that image and wondered what it could mean. So I asked:

What is a house of gloom?

How did it get that way?

Did someone die in the house?

How do people act in a gloomy house?

Is your own house ever gloomy?

What gloom do you have in your life?

What are you gloomy about?

What would you tell young children about a gloomy house?

And my answer is:

The House Of Gloom

N o one smiled in the House of Gloom
Not father, nor mother, nor sister Lyn, nor
baby John.
All were unhappy,
one could assume,
in that sad, sad House of Gloom.
Father's face was always long and stern
as if he felt impending doom
inside that dismal House of Gloom.
Every day the mother swept
dust into corners
with her witch's broom
in that dirty House of Gloom.
Sister Lyn would pout and shout.
And when nothing went right
all day she would fume
in that horrible House of Gloom.
Baby John would scream and cry
as he would fall from a chair
with a loud "Ka boom!"
In that noisy House of Gloom.
There was plenty of room
in that House of Gloom
for laughter, singing and dancing.
But all were too grumpy
in the unhappy House of Gloom.
Nothing else would live,
no plant, no flower,
not even a mouse
in that awful gloomy house.
The meals were silent
for bitterness and anger
was all they would consume
in that dark, dingy, House of Gloom.
If ever laughter was heard
the windows would be quickly shut
and the whole family would resume
their life in the House called Gloom.
Outside the weeds were tall

and never did a flower bloom
near the ugly House of Gloom.
People stayed far away
and no one dared near that spooky tomb
of the haunted House of Gloom.
The sun would never shine
from behind the heavy black cloud
that would always loom
over that morbid House of Gloom.
There was never gladness
but only sadness
in the darkness
of the House of Gloom.
Now, would you like to live
in such a terrible place
where no one would smile
and no one embrace?
Would you live in a gloomy house
without laughter and joy
and not even one little toy?
Be patient and kind
whatever you do
and share what you have with all those near you.
For one little smile
and one kind word
can be like sweet smelling perfume
to those who are dwelling in the dark House of Gloom.
Be happy and cheerful
to all that you meet.
And never be one for whom
is the dark House of Gloom.

* * *

COMMENTS:

"The House of Gloom" is not a prose story and, in fact, is not even a poetic story. Some people might even say this short work does not even qualify as poetry. I have included it here to give another example of a simple, creative expression which can be used for reflecting on a faith experience.

The fun part of composing this work came in reflecting on the word gloom. In thinking of the word gloom, the word doom immediately came to mind. As I thought more and more, other rhyming words came to mind, and ultimately came the description of what the house of gloom might be like.

The poetic description, like most of my stories, is first of all aimed at children and the child in everyone. The description attempts to capture a universal situation — we all seem to live in a gloomy house at one time or another, even if for just a short period of time.

This poetic description is perhaps more directly didactic than a story in that it presents a message at the end of what to do in order to avoid living in a gloomy house.

Although I have not yet had the opportunity, I think this work could be used well in a catechesis or liturgy for Penance. I think it would work well especially in a family situation as the characters in the house would provide a basis for each member of a family to reflect on how each contributes to the gloominess of the family.

This example of a different type of creative expression has been offered especially for those who might find composing prose stories difficult or too overwhelming a task. Maybe this example may encourage someone to create other types of poetic reflections. Maybe there is some situation, idea, object, or person which could be used as the basis for reflection and expressed poetically in a class or prayer service. Maybe someone might even be inspired to develop a prose story about the house of gloom.

Or, some other topic might form the basis for a poetic prayer, such as:

"In the city of joy,
there lived a boy ... "
or
"The miracle on the hill

which started with Phil ...
... until all ate their fill."
or whatever you might find, if you are not blind, to the images
of your mind ...

9. A LOVE STORY

To celebrate Confirmation in our parish, one must be at least a senior in high school. Because we deal basically with adults, our Confirmation program is less concerned with formal indoctrination than it is with faith sharing. Our sessions for the candidates are conducted in small groups which are facilitated by Confirmed adults.

One of the sessions deals with the Eucharist. The session begins with a pot luck dinner, each of the candidates bringing something to contribute. After the meal there is a consideration of the topic of the Eucharist.

Since the Eucharist is central to the faith life of the adult confirmed Roman Catholic, there is a real temptation in designing the program to want to tell the candidates everything we think they should know about the Eucharist. However, since the focus of the sessions is on faith sharing rather than lecture, real discipline is required to facilitate the sharing process in order to allow sufficient opportunity for the candidates to be able to express and deepen their own understanding about the Eucharist.

It would be fairly simple to use a series of a hundred and one discussion questions about the Eucharist which could ask the appropriate questions for discussing Eucharist. But my experience has been that these questions are often threatening, like, "What do you believe about the Eucharist?" Even the question, "What do you do with the Eucharist?" seems misdirected and often misunderstood.

So, in designing the Confirmation program I was challenged to use a story with the candidates about Eucharist. The problem with a story is that one becomes limited in one's approach to an idea. No story can be expected to cover all of the important aspects of any topic without becoming too long, confusing, and boring.

I decided to focus on the theme of love in the Eucharist. I chose as the backdrop for the story the common image of a fairy tale princess. In a fairy tale the princess always seems to fall in love and live happily ever after. Eucharistic love is something like that. The big problem for the fairy tale princess is how does she find Prince Charming? What criteria does she use? And what is the relationship between the way the fairy tale princess finds her prince and the lover in the Eucharist?

Since an important aspect of the Confirmation program is faith *sharing,* I was also challenged to develop a story which would be open-ended so as to allow for discussion and not just preach about Eucharist. Thus, the following attempt.

Three Loaves Of Bread

O nce upon a time there lived a beautiful young princess. She was the most beautiful, loving, and kind princess ever to have lived. And because she was so beautiful many young men desired to marry her. But the poor princess did not know which man she should marry.

There were three young men for whom the princess had a special affection and each of them desired to marry the beautiful princess. The princess decided that she would see if she should marry one of these three young men. So one day the lovely princess called the three young men to her castle in order to test them so that she could determine which, if any, she should marry.

The men who came at the call of the princess were royal, noble and brave. Their hearts were filled with love and each dreamed of being the one who would marry the beautiful girl and live happily ever after with her.

The beautiful princess told the three young men that she wondered if she were to marry any of them and that before she made up her mind the brave and noble men would have to prove their love for her.

The first prince immediately said that he would gladly slay a thousand dragons to prove his love for the young maiden. The second prince knelt before the beautiful girl and swore that he would easily swim the widest ocean if only that is what she desired. And the third prince promised the lovely princess his entire kingdom if she would only marry him.

But the beautiful young girl smiled and shook her head. No, that was not enough. For indeed there was more to love than all of that. So the princess said that she would give each prince a gift. And each prince was to return in exactly one week, with or without the gift, and tell the princess what he had done with the gift. When they returned with their answers, the princess would decide which one, if any, she would marry.

Now the gift that the fair maiden gave to each prince was not the type of gift one might expect from a princess. It was not the gift of a crown or expensive jewels. It was not the gift of a royal cape, nor was it a heavy shiny sword. No, instead, the gift the princess gave to each prince was an ordinary, common, freshly baked loaf of bread.

The bread was like ordinary bread in all ways but one. You see, the princess had baked this bread herself, and that was unusual for a princess who had servants, maids, and cooks to do her work for her. But the lovely young girl had made this bread with her own two gentle hands and baked it with her own loving care. And so, indeed it was a special gift to receive bread baked by a princess.

The three young noble men were surprised at the strange gift. Each was puzzled as he wondered what he should do with it in order to prove his love for the young woman.

The beautiful maiden told them one last thing as she gave them the loaves of bread. She instructed the men not to carry sword nor purse when they left the castle. They could only carry the bread. And she further instructed them to return with neither sword nor purse. Obediently and humbly the three young men did as the princess ordered them.

The first prince rode off to his kingdom in the west. When he reached his home he placed the freshly baked bread on his long dining table and then he sat down to contemplate the meaning of the strange gift.

The first prince thought, "Certainly this is a special bread for it was made by the very hands of the one I love. There is something of the princess herself in this bread," he reasoned. "What can I do with this bread," he wondered, "that would prove my love for her and make her want to marry me?"

Then the idea struck him. "Why, what else would one do with bread than to eat it? Yes," thought the prince, "to eat this bread would be like having a part of the princess herself. Oh, to taste the bread would be like tasting her!"

The prince decided he had to eat the bread, but not all at once, for that would be too much. So he carefully scored the bread so he would have seven slices, one for each day of the long week that he must wait until he could return to the castle where the young girl would most certainly decide to marry him because of his wisdom.

And so, each day of that long week the prince ate one slice of the deliciously baked bread. Each slice was a taste of love, each morsel was savored, and each day the first prince was filled with love for the beautiful princess.

On the seventh day the prince ate the last piece of bread. Every last crumb was eaten so there would be no waste of this precious gift. When the last tiny crumb had been eaten the prince set off on his journey back to the castle of the princess.

The second prince had taken his gift of the bread to his kingdom in the north. He guarded his bread carefully, keeping it warm by holding it tightly underneath his cloak. He rode his horse as fast as he could and he said not a word to anyone on his journey home.

When the second prince returned home he immediately locked his castle. Then he locked himself in his room and bolted it so tightly that no one else could enter. For the second prince had determined that this was such a special bread that he would not even allow anyone else to see it.

The prince adored the bread and kept it close to him at all times as a sign of the princess' love. He even began to think that perhaps there was something magical about the bread, and he dared not cut it for fear of having it lose its magical powers.

So the prince vowed that he would guard the bread, that he would not eat any piece of it until he was able to take it back to the princess and eat it with her in the queendom. The second prince even made a promise that he would eat nothing else that long week. Instead, he would fast and only look longingly at the bread, letting it be a reminder of his longing to be with the beautiful young girl forever.

The prince kept his vow and guarded that special bread for one long week. Each day his hunger grew and he longed to have just one small bite of the gift of the bread. But he was a strong and noble prince and he would not give in to any temptation. No, each pain in his stomach was instead a reminder of the burning love he had for the beautiful princess. "Oh," he thought to himself, "she will be so proud of my accomplishment, of my self-control and fortitude, that she will certainly marry me!"

The third prince had taken his gift of the bread to his kingdom in the east. But on his journey back to his kingdom the third prince stopped to water his horse at a running brook.

The third prince did not at first notice the woman who suddenly appeared from the thicket near the brook. He did not notice that she had taken off her long cape and stretched it out like a blanket on the tall green grass. But when the prince turned to mount his horse he did see her and he stopped to contemplate the sight.

The prince looked at the woman lying seductively on the silky red lining of her cape. Her hands were spreading out the long strands of her beautiful hair as if she were drying it in the warm sun. The prince gazed longingly at the woman for indeed she was a tempting woman for any man. But the prince was virtuous and noble and so the prince turned away and began to mount his horse.

But the woman called out sweetly to the young man, "Even the rider needs refreshment." The prince only shook his head and said nothing in reply.

The prince looked down at the woman and knew she probably could indeed make him happy. But as he looked at the woman he could only see the eyes of the beautiful young princess, and it was only her he desired. So the prince turned away and grabbed the reigns of his horse.

The woman immediately jumped up and grabbed the prince's leg. "Oh, please sir," she implored. "I'll do anything for you. All I ask is enough to buy food for my young child who has not eaten in many days."

As the prince looked down at the woman he saw tears streaming down her cheeks and he felt sorry for her. "I have no money to give you," he told her sadly. "All I have is this loaf of ... " He could not finish the sentence. The words stuck in his throat. "No! Not the bread! Not the precious gift from the beautiful princess!" he shouted to himself.

Then his heart sank. He was a noble and compassionate prince, but he did not know what to do. This bread was a gift! He could not just give it away to anyone, let alone give it to a woman who had to whore in order to feed her child. Oh, what would the princess say if he told her he had given the bread to a hungry woman. His head pounded and silent words screamed inside it.

Questions raced through the young man's mind as he tried to decide what he should do. If he did not give the woman the bread, she would be forced to search out another man and give herself to him so she could feed her hungry child. Maybe there wasn't a child ... but maybe there was.

The prince closed his eyes tightly in pain. He pictured the beautiful princess and then he heard the cry of hunger from a young child. Finally, the prince let out a loud scream of anguish which echoed throughout the countryside, and with a whack of his hand he sent his horse galloping from the bank of that brook.

The prince raced on at a feverish pace, leaving the woman lying in the dust caused by his racing horse. Within seconds the horse reached the top of the hill and the prince pulled the reigns for a quick stop. He turned and looked down at the woman near the brook. The prince clutched the loaf, digging his fingers into the soft freshly baked bread which the princess had given him. Then, with all the strength in his body, he threw the bread down the hill at the woman near the brook. He did not stay to hear any response for he galloped away as fast and as far as he could until his horse stopped from exhaustion.

The third prince spent the rest of his long week roaming the countryside slowly and crying until he had no more tears. For the prince realized that in giving away the bread he had given away his life. He knew the beautiful young princess would never marry him now.

On the seventh day the third prince made his arduous journey back to the castle of the princess. He came into her presence unkempt, disheveled, and sleepless. His heart was carried like a heavy stone within his body as he joined the two others who came excitedly to tell the princess what they had done with the gift of the bread.

The princess greeted the three young men and stood before them, looking more beautiful and dazzling than ever. She wore a white princess gown which was covered by a pale blue royal cape. Her princess crown sparkled brightly on her head and, indeed, she was the most beautiful princess ever to have lived.

The first prince knelt down eagerly before the young woman and anxiously told how he had carefully sliced the bread, eating only one piece each day as a reminder of the beautiful princess. Each day his love for the princess increased as he was nurtured by her wonderful gift.

Then the second prince knelt before the princess and excitedly told how he had not even dared to think about eating the bread, for it was much too precious a gift simply to be consumed like some common meal. Instead, he told how he had bravely guarded the special gift and how he had mortified himself so that he would be prepared to accept the gift of the princess herself in marriage.

Then the third prince knelt down but he kept his head hung

low, for he did not want the princess to see the horrible shame on his face. He mumbled his response so softly that the others could barely hear it as he told he had given the bread to a woman who was whoring so that she could feed her hungry child.

There was a gasp from the other two young men, but then there were snickers of relief, for they thought now they would only be in competition against each other for the maiden's hand. And each thought his response was better than the other's.

The beautiful young princess stood expressionless before the young men. She was silent for a long, long time as she carefully contemplated what each had done with the gift of the bread. She had to think long and hard, for hers was not an easy decision to make. Which, if any, of these three young noble men should she marry?

Then the beautiful young princess gave her answer to each man ...

* * *

Finish the story for yourself. Which, if any, of the three men would the princess decided to marry and why would she choose that man?

Turn the page for the ending I came up with ...

The beautiful young princess smiled lovingly as she spoke. "None of you had to tell me what you did with the bread for I already knew. For all of you were right, the bread was indeed special. I made it myself, and so I was a part of it and a part of all that you did with it."

Then the beautiful princess spoke to the first prince. "You were right in thinking that bread is to be eaten to provide nourishment. You sliced it carefully so you would have one piece for each day and now, at the end of the week, you have nothing left to give away. If I were to marry you, perhaps our lives would be the same. After a week we would have nothing left. No, prince, you only thought of yourself, and so I will not marry you."

Then the princess spoke to the second prince. "You were indeed noble and brave for you guarded the bread as something special, and you have mortified yourself in your longing for me. But look at what you have done. You have returned to me with a body which is weak and ill and will require nursing to make you strong again."

The second prince began to protest, wanting to tell the princess that he was strong, even stronger because of his mortification. But the princess interrupted his protest and continued speaking. "I gave you a freshly baked loaf of bread. Look at what you have brought back to me. It is a hard, crusty, stale loaf that now is only good for feeding to the birds. I don't want our love to become like that. And so, prince, I will not marry you either."

The princess knelt down before the third prince and held his head with her soft and gentle hands. "Third prince, you gave away the special gift." The maiden's words sounded like an eternal condemnation to the noble young man. "And in giving away that gift you knew you would be giving away your life and the life we could share together. That was indeed a noble and daring act."

The beautiful young princess stopped speaking and unclasped her flowing royal cape. She took the cape and draped it around the third prince. Through his tears the prince noticed that the cape was lined in silky red, and as the prince looked up into the eyes of the beautiful young princess he saw the eyes of a woman who needed bread for her starving child. And they lived happily ever after.

* * *

COMMENTS:

You may disagree with my ending of this story, and that's fine. The story was intended to provoke discussion, not to bring about a consensus. Numerous interpretations are possible, and each might express some aspect of what we believe about the Eucharist as Roman Catholics.

The first prince ate the bread, and the princess said he was right in saying bread was intended to be eaten. Within the last one hundred years the Roman Catholic Church has renewed its emphasis on eating the bread by encouraging people to receive the Eucharist. The lower age for the first reception of the Eucharist and the reduction of the Eucharistic fast are just two expressions of the belief that Eucharistic bread should be eaten. But only eating the bread limits the full expression of the Eucharist and thus, the princess did not marry the first prince.

The princess also stated that the second prince was correct in believing that the bread was special and that this bread should be respected. This is also a part of our belief about the Eucharist. However, at some points in history there has been excessive emphasis placed on the reverence for the bread which diminished the nurturing aspects of Eucharist. The second prince expressed this extreme preoccupation with reverence by his locking the doors and carefully guarding the bread, a bitter, stale, hard loaf which had not served the purpose for which it had been made. Thus, the princess did not marry the second prince.

The princess chose the third prince because she was directed, by the author, to see this as the best of the three Eucharistic meanings. The ending of the story expresses my own preference for placing emphasis on the sharing aspect of Eucharistic bread. The sharing also involved sacrifice, since the third prince thought because of the sharing he would certainly lose his chance to marry the princess. Sharing Eucharistic bread can be painful at times.

But, to be perfectly honest, I chose this ending only because I believe it is the best of the three choices, and also because the story is a fairy tale love story in which the prince and princess are supposed to live happily ever after. But I don't think the princess should have chosen the third prince.

The third prince came back empty handed, just like the first prince. And even thought the third prince somewhat understood the meaning of the sharing aspect of the bread, he took on too much self pity because of that sharing. Instead of spending his time feeling sorry for himself, the third prince should have spent his time baking another loaf, which he could have brought back as a gift to the princess. He could have returned joyfully to the princess, recounting how he had used her bread to help feed a hungry child, but now bringing a gift of himself in return to her. Or, he could have at least returned with the ingredients for making bread and wooing the princess with something like, "I gave your bread to a hungry child. Then I spent the rest of the week working in the fields, gathering the harvest to bring you grain for making more bread. For you are the only one who can make such special bread..."

That approach is perhaps the way we should respond with Eucharist bread. We should receive it as a gift, eat it, and take it as part of ourselves to nurture and feed others. But we should return again, after working the harvest, and say, "Here, Lord, only you can make this special bread, but I have brought something for you to use..."

However, that ending would have given the third prince an unfair advantage: it would have seemed obvious that he was going to be the winner. There may have been little discussion at the end of the story. I wanted the characters to be as equally matched as possible so some hard decisions would have to be made.

But discussion groups have even criticized the original ending, saying the third prince had an unfair advantage because it was only to him that the princess appeared. In fact, the first and the second princess may well have complained, "But princess, when did we see you?" It is an echo of the Gospel lament, "Lord, when did we see you...? The problem is that the princess really did not have an opportunity to appear to the first and second princess. They had hurried home and immediately locked themselves in their castles either to eat the bread or to guard it carefully. They did not take time to water their horses. Maybe the message for all eaters of the bread is that we should not just rush home after our weekly Liturgy but should take a slow ride and stop to water the horses so we might be more sensitive to the opportunities for sharing the bread.

One final note about my use of the three princes: trilogy creates a balance in a story. This is not a new technique. Most of us grew up with the three bears, the three little pigs, three blind mice, three little kittens. Even jokes often use the trilogy technique, such as, "There was a person from country A, a person from country B, and a person from country C ..." We know immediately when the story begins that the third character is going to get zapped and be the brunt of the joke. Jesus used this approach himself in the story of the good Samaritan, but he reversed the meaning, and the third character came out being the good guy!

10. CONCLUSION

Balloons, candy, toys, snowflakes, trees, stones, buses, doors, bread, Coke ... farmers, wedding feasts, vineyards, treasures, pearls, nets ... these are the things stories are made of. I hope you have been able to walk behind the cart of the pages of this modest work, and I hope you have already started to push the cart yourself and call out the good news of your faith in new and creative ways.

Throughout this book I have shared not only a variety of stories, but also the faith-experience from which the stories came and the faith-context in which they were or could be used. I have attempted to stir the creative spirit within the reader so the reader might be moved to compose and tell stories. I would like to summarize my own guidelines for composing and telling stories, realizing that these are guidelines to which I have not strictly adhered, even in this book. However, I generally try to follow these guidelines and present them here for whatever help they might give others.

Guidelines for composing Faith Stories

1) Pray with the scriptures constantly. If you want to share faith stories, the scriptures must be an important part of your life. Otherwise, your stories might be good stories, but they won't be faith stories.

In praying with the scriptures, let yourself enter into the stories. Take the part of different characters and stop the action in the story so you can create your own dialogue and action. There is a lot the Bible doesn't tell us. There is a lot of room for development. For instance, did you ever wonder what Zaccheus' wife said when Jesus, an unexpected guest, suddenly appeared for dinner? And what did Jesus and Zaccheus talk about during that dinner? How did it end?

In your praying with the scriptures focus on the images, such as water, mountains, trees, hands, and stones. Try to put yourself into their places and see what they see, hear what they hear, and speak what might be on their minds.

2) Read children's stories. Let yourself become a child again. Tell the stories to the child within you. Let the characters of your childhood fantasies speak to you in new ways. Let the images of your childhood fill your mind as they would the mind of a child.

3) Find a source of quick reading material for those short mental breaks we all need. You may not become a good creator of stories because of this, but you will excel at trivia games.

4) Question everything. Be attentive to your environment and daily experiences. Stop and ask, "What does this say about my faith?" What could I tell others about this experience? *How* would I tell others about it? How could I help a child to see this as a faith experience? What images would I use to help a child to understand?" Never be satisfied with an answer. Go on questioning.

5) Strip away some of your adult sophistication. Don't be afraid of talking trees or flying elephants, for they are the stuff of which stories are made.

6) Focus on single images and examine them completely. Whatever is done in the story should constantly draw attention to the image and its message.

7) Use simple language, and don't overdescribe. Compose the story so it could be understood and enjoyed by a first grader.

8) Avoid complicated dialogues and plots. These are for novels.

9) Don't moralize or tell the listeners what you think they should believe about the story. Let the story speak to the heart of the listener, and save the moralizing for a follow-up discussion.

10) Write and rewrite. Rewrite again. I have rewritten some

stories up to fifteen times before I was satisfied with them. And even now as I look back on these stories, I would like to continue to change parts.

Guidelines for Telling the Stories

1) Practice telling your story *before* you get in front of an audience.

2) *Tell* the story. Even a story which is read should be told from the heart. You must make the story come alive and be convinced of the story yourself before you can tell it to others.

3) Don't attempt to memorize a story word for word. Put the story into your own words so you are comfortable telling it. Even if you are using someone else's story, don't be afraid of using your own words to retell the story. Preoccupation with memorization can rob the story teller of vital energy which is needed for really making the story come alive.

4) Know your audience, and let them know you before you tell the story.

5) Maintain eye contact with your audience. Eyes are windows to the soul. The story should be coming from your soul, and you want to place the story within the audience's soul.

6) Don't hide behind a podium. Come on out to tell the story. But don't over act. Use enough drama to bring the story alive, but let the story speak, and don't draw attention to yourself. If you are prone to great gesticulation, you might be better at interpretive dance than story telling.

7) Be creative. Let the story serve you. Don't be a slave to the story. If you want to drop a scene or even change an ending, go ahead. Do whatever serves your purpose.

8) Think of ways of extending the story and making it become further part of the audience's experience. But be careful not to overdo a story or overteach it. Literary criticism is part of English 303, not faith sharing.

9) Approach the story as a gift to be given away. Don't be afraid of letting the audience take the story home. That's what you want them to do as a story teller. Don't be afraid of letting others end the story or of letting them draw different conclusions than yours.

10) Finally, whenever you tell a story, tell it *slowly*. Stories are like bananas. Only gorillas rip bananas apart. Civilized people peel bananas slowly, carefully, and deliberately. Do

likewise when you tell a story so the audience may gradually come to see the fruit which has been hidden by the skin. Then, like the banana, the story stands there for all to see, tempting to the taste. Bananas. You know, there might be a story there ...